There is nothing more powerful than starting your day with fresh jewels of wisdom to carry you through. Marilyn Gray, a prayer warrior for many years, provides those jewels and riches through her new devotional book, *Jewels of Wisdom*. One of the foundational principles of Restoring the Foundations is the ability to hear God's voice clearly. We have been in a ministry relationship with Wayne and Marilyn Gray since 2000 and as long as we have known Marilyn, she has always been a woman who has sought after God's heart. She has pressed in to know His voice and obey His Word. We know that *Jewels of Wisdom* was birthed out of that place of intimacy with the Lord, so please join us in sharing and celebrating these precious jewels from the Throne Room.

—Chester and Betsy Kylstra
Founders, Restoring the Foundations
Integrated Approach to Biblical Healing

I have always loved a good devotional and applaud Marilyn Gray for writing *Jewels of Wisdom*. What's most important to me is do I feel the anointing, the presence of God as I read—and I can answer that question with a "yes." Only a transformed life can produce transformation in another's, and *Jewels of Wisdom* was written out of the depths of her own relationship with the Lord. It's a great balance of revelation with practical application.

—Kathy S. Tolleson
www.OrganicMinistry.com
Author, *Prodigal Daughter* and *Redeemed*

JEWELS
OF
WISDOM

JEWELS
OF
WISDOM

MARILYN GRAY
FOREWORD BY BARBARA WENTROBLE

WinePressPublishing
Your Book, Defined. Since 1991.

ISBN 13: 978-1-4141-1793-5
ISBN 10: 1-4141-1793-0
Library of Congress Catalog Card Number: 2010904977

ACKNOWLEDGMENTS

THIS BOOK IS dedicated to my husband, Wayne. Not only have we been married for more than thirty years, but we have gone through the fire and have come out the other side not smelling like smoke. Wayne, you are my best friend and my greatest encourager. Knowing that you have always believed in me, and that you are the gift of God in my life, has meant everything to me. You have laid down your life for me so I could follow my dreams. I love you and will always be grateful and thankful that God brought us together for such a time as this. Ever since the first day I met you and knew in my heart we would be together, life with you has been amazing. Even in the roughest days and years, you never quit. Thank you. I love you with all of my heart.

Secondly, I want to thank my spiritual mom and dad, Mardel and David, for loving me through thick and thin. Your unconditional love and acceptance of me has brought so much healing into my life. God has used you in a mighty way to bring such joy and peace. You truly have been a mom and dad to me in more ways than you know. I don't know where I would be today if it wasn't for your love. You have believed in me, mentored me, and supported Wayne and me in our marriage when things were good and when things were bad. You never gave up on us. Thank you.

Thirdly, I want to thank my family and all the many friends who have walked with me in my journey of life. Caralee, Sandy, Marlene, David, and Mom—what an awesome family you are. Each one of you has touched my life in a very special and unique way. I am the woman I am today because of all we have gone through as a family. I will always have a special place in my heart for each one of you. I also want to thank my friends Gen, Gary, Danice, Don, Sherri, and especially my buddy and friend Judy, all the mentors and pastors who have poured their lives and wisdom into me. There are so many others I want to thank as well—you know who you are. I think I am the most blessed woman on this earth!

Last but not least, I want to thank those at the Northwest Christian Writer's Association and the team of Joyful Writers (Robin, April, and Lori) who helped me actually get this book published. You have believed in me and the calling on my life and helped me to fulfill my destiny. Thank you for everything.

Above all, I want this book to be dedicated to my Lord Jesus Christ. My life has been, and continues to be, dramatically transformed by Your love for me. Everything written in *Jewels of Wisdom* is to give You the glory!

FOREWORD

"TEACH MY PEOPLE to hear My voice." Those words spoke to my spirit loud and clear! Driving to a distant state with my husband and another couple was fun but would also turn out to be a tedious trip. We decided to quit talking and try to determine if the Lord had any instructions for us. As I quieted my mind and spirit, I sensed the Lord giving me a direction for my life. Life for me would never be the same after that day! My mandate in life would be to help teach God's people how to hear His voice.

Without an inner awareness of God's presence and voice, humankind would be left to its own crippled journey through life. Only God's voice and His wonderful nearness can give true meaning to life.

Numerous self-help books are available today. Seminars and conferences focus on ways to develop your strengths. Motivational speakers cause people to believe they can conquer the world—until they leave the meeting. Only as a person welcomes God's inner presence can the difficulties in his or her life be changed.

Marilyn Gray is a woman who has overcome powerful obstacles in life. She has pressed into God's presence and had her life transformed. Out of her own transformational experiences with the Lord, Marilyn is able to assist others as they are changed into their true purpose in life. Her book, *Jewels of Wisdom*, offers daily encouragement, strength, and a love that will transform your life!

Marilyn has discovered the secret to powerful living. She has a compelling mandate from the Lord. She has been called to help people break out of ordinary living and live life in God's supernatural presence.

Get ready to experience God in a new way. Get ready to live life in a new dimension. Get ready to allow the Lord to direct your path into your great destiny. You were born for this hour. Now enjoy your daily journey in life through the powerful devotions found in *Jewels of Wisdom*!

—Barbara Wentroble
President, International Breakthrough Ministries
President, Breakthrough Business Network
Author, *Prophetic Intercession*; *Rise to Your Destiny,*
Woman of God; *Praying With Authority*;
Removing the Veil of Deception

INTRODUCTION

> Blessed is the man who finds wisdom, the man
> who gains understanding, for she [wisdom] is more
> profitable than silver and yields better returns than
> gold. She is more precious than rubies; nothing you
> desire can compare with her.
>
> —Proverbs 3:13–15

THE WRITER OF Proverbs encourages us to seek diligently for wisdom. I have come to understand that wisdom is attained by those who are hungry and thirsty for more, and those who are determined to find it. Once found, wisdom is filled with truth and love. In my personal experience, searching for wisdom was actually a search for God Himself.

My journey began at a young age. I was born in a home where healthy relationships did not exist due to verbal, mental, and physical abuse; and I often felt unsafe and unprotected. From an early age, I sought something, anything, to make me feel safe. Once I was grown and out of the house, I began a successful career in real estate. Even though I was looking good on the outside—young and beautiful, bright and cheery, smart and intelligent, faithful and a hard worker—I was dying on the inside. I didn't know who I was. I became what others wanted me to be so somehow, some way, I would feel loved. As I fell deeper and deeper into despair and insecurity, I looked to the world to satisfy those needs. Work, money, alcohol, drugs, sex—anything to avoid feeling pain. At the same time, there was a knowing inside that there was a greater love available to me.

Today, I am a cancer survivor, delivered alcoholic and addict, and healed and whole all because of my relationship with Jesus Christ. Being reborn has forever changed my life. From the moment I accepted the Lord as my Savior, I began to hear Him speak to me. For the next three days—day in and day out—I journaled the words He spoke to me about my life. Everywhere I went, everything I heard, everything I saw was different. Over the years, I worked past the feelings of shame and unworthiness and began to really tap into the one, true love of God. I was on the path of healing and wholeness.

Looking back over my life, I see there were times when I felt I was definitely connected to God and could hear His voice in my heart. I recognized that whenever I was about to do something, I would get this sense of knowing—knowing if it was the right thing or a check in my heart if it was the wrong thing. I didn't know if it was just my imagination or if it was God leading me.

But I've come to know that it was, and is, God's voice. Over the years I have longed to know God's voice and let Him direct my steps and life. I've wanted to know Him, and I've wanted Him to know me.

Today, my relationship has grown to a place where even in circumstances of worldly sadness He continues to bring me joy. I know that through God I can always access that joy and hope. All I have to do is reach out to Him and then be still enough to hear His voice. I've come to know He cares for me and is always available.

God's desire is that you too would hear and know His voice.

The following compilations, or *Jewels of Wisdom*, are those He has spoken to my heart as I have walked with Him. My complete obedience to God is the reason I wrote this devotional. On January 27, 2003, on a plane from Seattle to Memphis, I heard the Lord's voice say to me, "Write your book. That will be the vehicle I use to catapult you into a traveling minister—a teacher of righteousness." I was swarmed with the old feelings of unworthiness. My first thought was, *Oh, how could I? I am not a journalist—I am afraid—it's a huge project. I want to be obedient, but how?* He said, "One day at a time, little by little, step by step, I will lead you. Begin with your journals; you have everything you need. Most people write books to tell their story. I want you to write a book about My story in you. A book of hope, a book of love, a book that will glorify Me. A tool to be like a double-edged sword to void hopelessness and bring joy—joy of Me, love of Me—to their hearts. I've given it to you; you have all you need. Do not let it be a burden, but let it be one of great rest and total immersion into My presence."

The Lord said, "Are you ready?"

I said, "Yes."

He said, "Well, let's get going."

This devotional is the first of two books.

I am a woman after God's heart and I desire to be close to Him. Today, He is my friend, comforter, confidant, counselor, travel agent, Savior, and, more than anything in the world, my Father. I want to share Him with you. As I've journaled during the last two decades, God has ministered to me and brought me healing, and I have gained revelation and wisdom from those conversations with Him. I am so grateful that He found me when I was lost. I am thankful He healed me when I was sick, and I am grateful He delivered me from my addictions. Now I am addicted only to Him and amazed by the depth of His love for me!

As you meditate on these words from God's heart, my hope is you will get to know my best friend. God loves to speak to His children, and He already considers you His friend. Let these words speak to you daily, encouraging you of His love and purpose for your life.

JANUARY

January 1

DON'T START THIS year out afraid. Read My Word, hear My Word, and do My Word. Come back to your first love. I have much to say to you, so open up your heart to receive it. This is the time to leave the past in the past and not carry the burdens into the new year. Use your past only as a marker, not as an identity. It comes down to a simple choice, and sometimes it is that easy. Know you are loved, sheltered, and guided each day. Just as a father holds his child's hand, let My hands hold you and walk with Me. Resign all rights to yourself. Give Me your time, talents, past, present, and future. Surrender it all.

Humble yourselves, therefore, under God's mighty hand, that he may lift you up in due time. Cast all your anxiety on him because he cares for you.

—1 Peter 5:6–7

January 2

Know My love for you in a new fresh way. Know that I AM for you and not against you. All that you need or will ever need, I have. I AM all you desire and all your heart seeks for. I created it that way—to desire Me more than you desire anything else. Whatever draws you away from Me will always cause you to stumble and can lead to the death of the promises I have for you. Remember, I AM the way, the truth, and the life. It is a narrow gate, but it is a path that always brings peace. Trust Me.

Enter through the narrow gate. For wide is the gate and broad is the road that leads to destruction, and many enter through it. But small is the gate and narrow the road that leads to life, and only a few find it.

—Matthew 7:13–14

January 3

I AM here for you always—during the storms, during the dark hours, in the midst of it all. Call out My name. I hear the faintest call. Take time to be with Me during the day. Notice the life that has been created all around you—in the sky, in a flower, in a smell. Notice these things. I AM the creator of all things. You can be assured that I care about you and all your needs as well.

> Then the LORD will appear over them; his arrow will flash like lightning. The Sovereign LORD will sound the trumpet; he will march in the storms of the south, and the LORD Almighty will shield them.
> —Zechariah 9:14–15

January 4

Press past the pain, press past the hurts—don't run back to the things that kept you in bondage. Never let the senses of past failures defeat your next step. Don't give up before the miracle happens. Don't give up too soon. Get up and do the next thing. Sing a new song and do what My book says. Be salt and light to the world and hoard nothing. Follow Me in sacrifice and in yielding to My Spirit. Come to the end of yourself. Seek holiness that results in your wholeness. Yes, there have been hard times, good times, fast times, and slow times. Time is in My hands. Remember, I cause all things to work together for good to those who love Me, to those who are called according to My purposes.

> Moses replied: "It is not the sound of victory, it is not the sound of defeat; it is the sound of singing that I hear."
> —Exodus 32:18

January 5

Trust in Me alone. You have tried to do things on your own. You have worshipped idols. When times are tough and you feel your heart sinking, lift your eyes and voice to Me. Any idols will not save you—actually, they pull you away from Me. Oh, that you would only know in your heart that I AM the way, the truth, and the life—nothing else can save you. I knew you before I formed you in your mother's womb, and I have set you apart. Nothing else will satisfy you. Turn from your ways and follow Me. You can trust My leading.

> Before I formed you in the womb I knew you, before you were born I set you apart; I appointed you as a prophet to the nations.
> —Jeremiah 1:5

January 6

Let Me mold you and shape you. Let Me do the work that needs to be done. Sometimes I will deliver you and sometimes I will take you through. Trust in Me. I want you to be sharp and ready—so be sure to discipline and perfect yourself. All thoughts that are harmful must be tuned out. Let Me expand your tent pegs as you spend time in fellowship with Me. I made you so I could love you because I AM love. Receive that today because you are in My care.

This is what the LORD says—he who made you, who formed you in the womb, and who will help you: Do not be afraid, O Jacob, my servant, Jeshurun, whom I have chosen.

—Isaiah 44:2

January 7

Withdraw from hurting others and let go of negativity. In order to multiply your joy, count your blessings. Sometimes I speak in silence, so be sure to be with Me rather than do for Me. I AM your friend and I will satisfy every part of your life. It's OK to be angry with Me. Just talk to Me—it's a way we can develop a deeper relationship.

In his hand is the life of every creature and the breath of all mankind.

—Job 12:10

January 8

Look forward to your home ahead in heaven and you will desire the world less. Be a living sacrifice. Keep your heart cleansed from offense and unforgiveness. I will give you peace in the midst of your difficulties. Trust Me with those situations. Overcome evil with good and press through any pain and discomfort. The important thing is your growth, and what you *feel* is unimportant. I AM looking for My image in you, and it's not found in your comfort.

In everything I did, I showed you that by this kind of hard work we must help the weak, remembering the words the LORD Jesus himself said: "It is more blessed to give than to receive."

—Acts 20:35

January 9

Deal with your own sin and don't be an expert in pointing out the sins of others. Judge not, that you be not judged. The broad way leads to destruction, but the narrow way leads to life. I want you to be calm; rest in Me. Don't strain and don't carry the burdens of yesterday. Give them to Me. Let Me search your heart, let Me cleanse the recesses of your heart that you don't see. I want you to walk in the light as I AM in the light. Don't worry about tomorrow or the results of anything, just obey Me. True obedience leads to success—I will be responsible from that point on. Be obedient to My calling on your life.

Trust in the LORD with all your heart and lean not on your own understanding; in all your ways acknowledge him, and he will make your paths straight. Do not be wise in your own eyes; fear the LORD and shun evil. This will bring health to your body and nourishment to your bones.

—Proverbs 3:5–8

January 10

The world is watching you—be sure to walk in purity and obedience. Your words and actions all have eternal value and they have influence forever and ever. Give up your right to yourself and entirely set yourself apart to the ministry of God's people. Make sure to be other-directed and other-compelled—put the self-life to death. To look inward is fatal, so always look upward to Me. Your salvation and your life are under grace.

> And as Christ's soldier, do not let yourself become tied up in worldly affairs, for then you cannot satisfy the one who has enlisted you in his army. Follow the LORD's rules for doing his work, just as an athlete either follows the rules or is disqualified and wins no prize. Work hard like a farmer who gets paid well if he raises a large crop.
>
> —2 Timothy 2:4–6 TLB

January 11

Put no other gods before Me—worship Me alone. At times when there is silence, I want you to draw upon the words I have spoken to you. You may have the consciousness of My presence but yet hear no voice. Abide in My presence anyway. You cannot escape discipline—it's My way of discipling you so you can disciple others. Don't run—don't rebel. Come to Me, My precious one. Just obey and leave the consequences to Me. Put no confidence in the flesh. Always trust Me in people around you, and don't look at their faults—look at their potential.

He has kept this secret for centuries and generations past, but now at last it has pleased him to tell it to those who love him and live for him, and the riches and glory of his plan are for you Gentiles, too. And this is the secret: Christ in your hearts is your only hope of glory.

—Colossians 1:26–27 TLB

January 12

Be glad, rejoice, say thank you. Use all I give you and give it away to help others. Don't be lukewarm. At times you may say you're rich and have need of nothing, but you are poor and blind. Those I love, I rebuke and chasten. As you repent and overcome, your life will be full of peace and victory, and you won't ever turn back. Stay teachable and walk away from any pride. The power of the cross or the power of sin—you choose what dominates.

Those who belong to Christ have nailed their natural evil desires to his cross and crucified them there. If we are living now by the Holy Spirit's power, let us follow the Holy Spirit's leading in every part of our lives.

—Galatians 5:24–25 TLB

January 13

I AM everything you need. At times I take away because I don't want you to be earthbound or self-reliant. I don't want anything to come between you and Me. Make right those things that need to be corrected and forget those things in the past. Press through with confidence and trust in Me. My strength is available to you to conquer anything that binds you. My name is above all other names—call on Me. Get alone with Me. Let Me deal with your soul so you can walk in the Spirit. My power is available to you.

> Brethren, I do not count myself to have apprehended; but one thing I do, forgetting those things which are behind and reaching forward to those things which are ahead, I press toward the goal for the prize of the upward call of God in Christ Jesus. Therefore let us, as many as are mature, have this mind; and if in anything you think otherwise, God will reveal even this to you. Nevertheless, to the degree that we have already attained, let us walk by the same rule, let us be of the same mind.
>
> —Philippians 3:13–16 NKJV

January 14

I AM so glad you spend time with Me in the morning. It makes Me smile that you put Me first each day. Make a conscious choice to kill self—I will give you power and you will be victorious. Sit in My presence, respond to My call. You are chosen for greatness. Be ready—say, "Here I am, Lord. Send me." Get over dead works. A warrior who enters a battle overloaded and weary is already defeated. Don't gather worldly things—seek only kingdom things.

> But seek first his kingdom and his righteousness, and all these things will be given to you as well. Therefore do not worry about tomorrow, for tomorrow will worry about itself. Each day has enough trouble of its own.
>
> —Matthew 6:33–34

January 15

As you read My Word, let it transform you. As you let My Word work in you, you will become more Christlike. Be a doer of the Word and not just a hearer. Do not let the problems of the world around you make you weary. Come and drink the Living Water for replenishment of your soul. Stop striving—I AM looking for obedience rather than sacrifice. Death to self means to stop striving. Rest in Me.

> Samuel replied, "Has the LORD as much pleasure in your burnt offerings and sacrifices as in your obedience? Obedience is far better than sacrifice. He is much more interested in your listening to him than in your offering the fat of rams to him."
>
> —1 Samuel 15:22 TLB

January 16

Watch your mouth—the tongue of the wise promotes health. Always speak the truth, be open and unafraid, never lie. I AM part of the little things in life as well as the big things. Persevere no matter what. Don't seek others' opinions regarding My call on your life—you will know My call because you will know the One who called. Listen—be attuned to Me. Do not worry about finances you need. Your need is supplied according to My riches in glory. Go in obedience and do not worry—there is more than enough.

> And it is he who will supply all your needs from his riches in glory because of what Christ Jesus has done for us.
>
> —Philippians 4:19 TLB

January 17

Don't be casual in your worship. Worship Me with all your heart and give Me your all. Abide in My love. Let Me surround you with My love. Give Me your heart, trust, and faith in all the circumstances you face. Don't worry. Love will cover a multitude of sins. Love Me, love others—that is your greatest commandment in this world. Receive My love and then be willing to give it away.

"Love the LORD your God with all your heart and with all your soul and with all your mind and with all your strength." The second is this: "Love your neighbor as yourself." There is no commandment greater than these.

—Mark 12:30–31

January 18

When you step out in faith, at times you will feel helpless. But faith without works is dead. So know I AM with you as you walk in faith. Do not doubt. Walk in obedience—do not be deceived by what the world would say or do; walk in My ways only. Do not let anything compete with your loyalty to Me. Do not let any distractions pull you away from spending time with Me. I AM your source of power!

And the disciples were continually filled with joy and with the Holy Spirit.

—Acts 13:52 NASB

January 19

Peace, peace, peace. Receive it, walk in it, sow it. Make a choice to walk in it—it is available to you any time. Expect it, anticipate it. My love, peace, and joy are yours for the asking. Try not to get ahead of Me; wait even if it's uncomfortable. Wait for the right time.

You will know when to move ahead and when to wait. Rely on Me and drop your plans. My plans and ways are higher than yours. Don't direct your own path—I promise to do that for you.

> In all your ways acknowledge Him, and He shall direct your paths. Do not be wise in your own eyes; fear the LORD and depart from evil.
> —Proverbs 3:6–7 NKJV

January 20

Think of Me, be one with Me. What you treasure, your heart will be there also. What is it that you treasure? Are you weak? Are you troubled? Are you confused? In your weakness I can give you strength, for it is made perfect in weakness. So let My grace be more than sufficient for you. My supply is never ending and it never runs out. Come to Me.

> And He said to me, "My grace is sufficient for you, for My strength is made perfect in weakness." Therefore most gladly I will rather boast in my infirmities, that the power of Christ may rest upon me.
> —2 Corinthians 12:9 NKJV

January 21

Seek Me, seek to be in My presence. Don't miss opportunities that come your way that would give us time to be together. Sing a song of praise and rejoice in this day. Be calm—all is well, for I AM with you. Don't ever forget what I have done for you. Always return to your first love—oh, how I desire to be with You. The broken world needs Me, and you are My vessel to bring hope, encouragement, and the Good News. Be a pure vessel I can work through—cleanse yourself from all impurities. Stay connected to Me and to others.

> Go now, leave your bonds and slavery. Put Babylon and all it represents far behind you—it is unclean to you. You are the holy people of the LORD; purify yourselves, all you who carry home the vessels of the LORD.
>
> —Isaiah 52:11 TLB

January 22

Let your light shine. Do not fear persecution. Tell people around you about the hope in your life. Be a witness for Me. Be thankful at all times—in all situations. It is a part of your training as My disciple. There are good days and bad days, but always say, "Thank You" in the midst of your day. It will get you through and you will be victorious. Look to Me—keep your eyes focused on Me.

Let us hold fast the confession of our hope without wavering, for He who promised is faithful.

—Hebrews 10:23 NKJV

January 23

Walk in obedience to what My Word says—walk in obedience in those things I tell you. There is freedom in obedience, not burden. My laws and commandments are in place to bring you safety, protection, direction, and guidance as you walk with Me. If you believe in Me, you will love Me and obey Me. Come and dwell in My presence. Be quiet, listen, and obey. Transformation will occur. Remember to take up your cross and follow Me—there is victory in the cross.

Now the LORD is the Spirit; and where the Spirit of the LORD is, there is liberty. But we all, with unveiled face, beholding as in a mirror the glory of the LORD, are being transformed into the same image from glory to glory, just as by the Spirit of the LORD.

—2 Corinthians 3:17–18 NKJV

January 24

Keep the faith. Finish the race with joy. Do not be concerned about today's events; they are grafted into My great plan. Stay steadfast and do not waiver. Joy, joy, joy is yours. I AM with you, even if you feel weak today. Take a step toward Me. Come and be in relationship with Me. Know Me and you know My purpose in your life. Take one step at a time. I AM waiting for you.

> We are praying, too, that you will be filled with his mighty, glorious strength so that you can keep going no matter what happens—always full of the joy of the LORD, and always thankful to the Father who has made us fit to share all the wonderful things that belong to those who live in the Kingdom of light.
> —Colossians 1:11–12 TLB

January 25

Leave behind material things—put no other gods before Me. Be generous in your giving. Give all that you have and all that you are. I AM a God of multiplication—I will multiply the little you have. I will direct your steps, so rest assured that I AM with you along this path of life. Open up your heart and see what lies dormant. I desire that you have a glad heart, a loving heart, and a cheerful heart, as it is good medicine. Life is to be lived to its fullest.

> Each man should give what he has decided in his heart to give, not reluctantly or under compulsion, for God loves a cheerful giver.
> —2 Corinthians 9:7

January 26

There's a time for rest, a time to pray, a time to go, and a time to stay. I have spoken to you about your future; I have spoken to you about the plan. Now is the time for taking action and moving forward. There have been storms in your past and there will be storms again, but remain calm. Remain calm in the midst of the storms. As you abide in Me, I will abide in you. Separate yourself from your worries and cares and from your own agenda. Consecrate those to Me and don't doubt. Let My reflection and glory be on your face so those around you will see a living God.

> But we Christians have no veil over our faces; we can be mirrors that brightly reflect the glory of the LORD. And as the Spirit of the LORD works within us, we become more and more like him.
>
> —2 Corinthians 3:18 TLB

January 27

Don't blame, don't complain, call on Me. You may think that life will always be this way, but do not despair. I AM in the midst of changing the bitter to sweet. Trust in Me. I AM your Rescuer—do not worry. There are things you don't fully understand, so put your trust in Me. Do not be moved by the pressure. Stand.

The LORD God is my strength; He will make my feet like deer's feet, and He will make me walk on my high hills.

—Habakkuk 3:19 NKJV

January 28

Come to Me in prayer. Gather together in prayer. Prayer is the vehicle to help others if you can't be there. I hear your prayers. Answers are on their way. In the world you will have trials and tribulations, but be of great cheer as I have overcome the world. Have the heart of a servant. Serve others instead of wanting to be served. Give and it will be given to you. Whether that's a prayer, a hug, food, a smile—anything—I say give. I so desire that you come to Me. Delight in Me as I delight in you. Spend a lot of time with Me—not with lists of things you want or need, but come just so you can delight in Me. Be in perfect oneness with Me. My ways are not your ways. Come, My little one.

I have told you these things, so that in me you may have peace. In this world you will have trouble. But take heart! I have overcome the world.

—John 16:33

January 29

Submit your will to Me. Your will needs to be surrendered. As you walk your walk, make sure to walk in truth and in love. Let nothing in your heart be troubled. If there are situations between you and your brothers and sisters, don't ignore them—go make them right. You be the first. Have no fear—all is well. I AM in charge; I see the beginning and the end. Trust in My guidance and have faith that all is well. Restore your relationships. It's the only way to love the way I love, and it's the fulfillment of My commandment.

> I desire to do your will, O my God; your law is within my heart.
>
> —Psalm 40:8

January 30

Don't be in a hurry. I know the demands of life are great right now, but rest in My peace, joy, and comfort. There are things I AM asking you to do today that only can be done as you fill up your spirit with Me. I will give you the strength and guidance you need and don't try to do it in your own strength. I would much rather you come and drink of the Living Water, eat of My Word, be renewed and strengthened. I have called you to a mighty work that only can be done in My power. Rest assured, in My timing all things will be accomplished. Slow down to listen. I AM with you right now. Slow down.

If you love me, obey me; and I will ask the Father and he will give you another Comforter, and he will never leave you. He is the Holy Spirit, the Spirit who leads into all truth.

—John 14:15–17 TLB

January 31

I AM your Redeemer. I AM the God of redemption. I will restore the years the locusts have eaten. I will redeem those things that have been lost. Your guarantee of a life that is full, rewarding, and satisfying is in Me. At times you may ask and wonder, *Where are You, God?* Well, I tell you I AM right here, right now in the midst of your life. There are things that you do not know right now, but I assure you that if you abide in Me, I will abide in you. Trust that I have your best interests in My heart. You can only see in part, but know that I AM with you no matter where you are. Lift up your hands to Me, let Me guide your feet, and keep your heart on Me.

Christ redeemed us from the curse of the law by becoming a curse for us, for it is written: "Cursed is everyone who is hung on a tree." He redeemed us in order that the blessing given to Abraham might come to the Gentiles through Christ Jesus, so that by faith we might receive the promise of the Spirit.

—Galatians 3:13–14

FEBRUARY

February 1

OBEDIENCE WILL BRING you peace. Obedience will bring you joy. Do not resist My hand, My Word, My promptings. Obedience brings blessings. I want to bless glad and thankful hearts. Do not worry about what the future holds. Lift up My name to a lost and broken world. Let your life be one that emanates My life. Let the fruit of the Spirit live in every cell of your body. Show the world there is a better way to live by the way you live. Let your life be one of good news to a lost and sinking world. I need you to pour out My love to others. Will you?

Let them do good, that they be rich in good works, ready to give, willing to share, storing up for themselves a good foundation for the time to come, that they may lay hold on eternal life.

—1 Timothy 6:18–19 NKJV

February 2

Forgive. Love. Don't hold onto offense. Always have a forgiving heart toward others. Remember how much I have forgiven you. You must offer it to others. Walk in love, give love. Those who want to be around you will be those who feel the most loved by you. Never hesitate to give it away. My love endures forever and it is yours for the asking. Do not keep it to yourself, though. I can always be found to replenish your supply of love—just call on Me and ask.

A new command I give you: Love one another. As I have loved you, so you must love one another. By this all men will know that you are my disciples, if you love one another.

—John 13:34–35

February 3

Are you willing to give Me the glory? Are you willing no matter what to let people see the conquering spirit within you? I AM that Conqueror. It's not what you have or haven't done; it's My overcoming power in you that causes you to overcome. Remember, when in the depths of affliction, submit to My will. Rely on every word I tell you. Let My love fill your heart. As you go from glory to glory, remember I AM your strength, I AM your provider, I AM that Conqueror to help and guide you along the way. My power is made strong in weakness.

> For the foolishness of God is wiser than man's wisdom, and the weakness of God is stronger than man's strength.
>
> —1 Corinthians 1:25

February 4

My power is endless. Victory is yours. Do not depend on anything but Me to hold you up. Believe in Me. Follow Me. Be My disciple. One I can train. My power is yours—do not put limits on it. Do not doubt—do not question. Stand in your authority—move in confidence—go forth—the victory is yours.

> I have given you authority to trample on snakes and scorpions and to overcome all the power of the enemy; nothing will harm you.
>
> —Luke 10:19

February 5

Trust in My love. Nothing will be accomplished by worrying. Worry is wasted time. If you have questions about life, ask Me. If you are hurting, fearful, and uncertain—ask Me. Give Me your feelings—pour them out on My shoulder. I want to hear from you.

> Then Jesus said to his disciples: "Therefore I tell you, do not worry about your life, what you will eat; or about your body, what you will wear."
> —Luke 12:22

February 6

Put away old things of the past. Put away those things that have been a distraction, a decoy, a desire of old ways of thinking or being. You must be willing to be placed on the altar and go through the fire. Put your focus on Me and nothing else. Put on the new man; I long to be with you. Come and be with Me not for what I can give you but just to sit in My presence.

> But now you must rid yourselves of all such things as these: anger, rage, malice, slander, and filthy language from your lips. Do not lie to each other, since you have taken off your old self with its practices and have put on the new self, which is being renewed in knowledge in the image of its Creator.
> —Colossians 3:8–10

February 7

Say yes to Me in whatever I want you to do. Do not focus on self. I can give you the answers if you would just ask. Trust Me and trust My Word. Do not be afraid. I know your sufferings and I hear your cries. I AM your light in a dark place. I will guide you with My light.

> Your word is a lamp to my feet and a light for my path.
>
> —Psalm 119:105

February 8

Do not get too far out ahead of Me and then forget Me. When things are going great, it's easy to get prideful and forget about Me. Be very cautious—remember, pride goes before a fall. Remain humble in all that you do. In all things I AM your supply. Endure with power. Be focused on My point of view. Let My nature control you.

> Pride goes before destruction, a haughty spirit before a fall.
>
> —Proverbs 16:18

February 9

Worship Me—always make time to worship Me. Don't get so busy doing the work for My sake and forget that your own heart must be filled. Make sure to be replenished and filled up. Take all the time you need. It's very important that you allow the oil to fill up your emptiness so you pour out in My anointing and not in your own strength. My anointing will break bondage. Worship Me in a new way today and let Me fill you up to overflowing.

> And as for you, the anointing which you received from Him abides in you, and you have no need for anyone to teach you; but as His anointing teaches you about all things, and is true and is not a lie, and just as it has taught you, you abide in Him.
> —1 John 2:27 NASB

February 10

My wounds have healed you. I bore your sins on the cross. I took them so you would live and live in righteousness. Your victories in those things that trouble you have already been nailed to the cross. Grace, grace, grace is yours. Freedom from bondage is yours. I AM your Savior. Bring all your thoughts into captivity and let Me transform your mind. My thoughts are not your thoughts. I have higher thoughts and plans for you. Receive your healing today.

Who Himself bore our sins in His own body on the tree, that we, having died to sins, might live for righteousness—by whose stripes you were healed. For you were like sheep going astray, but have now returned to the Shepherd and Overseer of your souls.

1 Peter 2:24–25 NKJV

February 11

Put the kingdom of God first. Quit worrying about your life—I have a plan. Prayer is your most powerful weapon. Lift up your prayers to Me. Remember to stay in your warrior stance and put on the armor of God and never cease to pray. Stay still, stay quiet, don't get too busy—slow down and listen to Me. Turn your eyes upon Me. Don't worry about time. Everything is in My hands.

For the kingdom of God is not a matter of eating and drinking, but of righteousness, peace and joy in the Holy Spirit, because anyone who serves Christ in this way is pleasing to God and approved by men.

—Romans 14:17–18

February 12

When you wake up, be aware of the sunrise. When you go to bed, be aware of the sunset. Stop, look, and breathe in the magnificent works of My hands. I have created all things for your great pleasure. Watch, see, and hear Me. Listen to Me rather than listen to My servants. Do not compare yourselves with others—keep focused and hear My words. Follow Me. Stop and listen—can you hear Me?

> Also your people shall all be righteous; they shall inherit the land forever, the branch of My planting, the work of My hands, that I may be glorified.
> —Isaiah 60:21 NKJV

February 13

Consider My love for you. Embrace the truth that My perfect love casts out all fear. My death on the cross was out of My love for My Father but also My love for you. Finish the race you have begun. Keep your eyes on the goal. I AM right here, by your side, to tackle anything that would try to hold you back.

> There is no fear in love; but perfect love casts out fear, because fear involves torment. But he who fears has not been made perfect in love. We love Him because He first loved us.
> 1 John 4:18–19 NKJV

February 14

Return to your first love—the Lover of your soul. Abide in My love. Sit at My feet. Your greatest work is to sit in My presence—above all. Ask of Me what you will. Be bold and courageous to speak love—the love I pour out on you—to others. I created you to give and receive love. Give it freely—do not hold back.

> I love the LORD, for he heard my voice; he heard my cry for mercy. Because he turned his ear to me, I will call on him as long as I live.
>
> —Psalm 116:1–2

February 15

Where are you in My kingdom? Do you know My power? Remember that no kingdom can stand that is divided upon itself. Is there division in your life? Repent, for God's kingdom is at hand. I AM with you always. Do not let your heart be hardened or allow strongholds to be built in your mind. Open up your understanding—let the outpouring of My Spirit fall upon you. Seek My kingdom and righteousness. It will never fail you.

> Jesus knew their thoughts and said to them, "Every kingdom divided against itself will be ruined, and every city or household divided against itself will not stand."
>
> —Matthew 12:25

February 16

What is your mouth saying? Is it in line with your heart or is it critical and judgmental of others? Speak blessings and not curses. The tongue is the ship's rudder and can turn away your destiny and promises from the highest plan I have for you. The mouth speaks out of the heart's issues, so have a checkup on your heart. Let the Great Physician perform surgery so that anything spoken will be pure and loving. Sometimes old habits are hard to break, but come to the One who can break the habits and perform miracles on your tongue.

> Keep your tongue from evil and your lips from speaking lies. Turn from evil and do good; seek peace and pursue it.
>
> —Psalm 34:13–14

February 17

Trust Me. Trust Me with the big things and trust Me with the small things. Trust in My love and trust in My direction. Trust in what you hear from Me. I will not lead you astray. Trust in those I have put in your life. Trust and faith go together. Trust in My unfailing love for you. Trust in My deliverance. Trust in My plans. Trust in My ways. Trust Me at all times.

Trust in Him at all times, you people; pour out your heart before Him; God is a refuge for us.

—Psalm 62:8 NKJV

February 18

My grace is sufficient for you. Don't rely on idols and forfeit the grace that is yours. Grace and peace go hand in hand. Where there has been sin, grace has abounded that much more. Grace is a gift—receive it freely. There is nothing you can do to earn grace. At times you may have felt unworthy to receive it, but it is yours anyway. Don't live by worldly wisdom but live by grace. Grace is freely given. In Me you have redemption through My blood and the forgiveness of sins in accordance with the riches of God's grace, which I lavish on you with all wisdom and understanding.

But by the grace of God I am what I am, and his grace to me was not without effect.

—1 Corinthians 15:10

February 19

No service for Christ will go unnoticed. I see your heart, I see the hard work, I take notice. Endure to the end. Many get weary and quit. Don't ever quit. I AM here, I AM listening to your prayers—they are not going unheard. I AM in the transforming and restoring business. You might not see or understand My ways, but they will never lead you astray. Rest in Me. Rest in what I have for you. Do not question or doubt My ways. I love you and will always love you. Be assured of that.

> Will your courage endure or your hands be strong in the day I deal with you? I the LORD have spoken, and I will do it.
> —Ezekiel 22:14

February 20

I AM not bound by your limitations or boundaries. I AM not limited by your expectations. I AM the source of all your dreams, hopes, and joys. Come and lay your petition down. Whatever you ask in My name, I will do. I desire to give you the best. I delight in you as you delight in Me. Come and abide.

> And I will do whatever you ask in my name, so that the Son may bring glory to the Father. You may ask me for anything in my name, and I will do it.
> —John 14:13–14

February 21

Be a vehicle of hope to others. Your hope is in Christ, your hope is in Me. There are many blinded, hurting, and hopeless people who need a touch from the Master. Go and tell them the good news. Hope is Having Options to Praise Everything. Tell them to flee from all evil and pursue righteousness, godliness, faith, love, endurance, and gentleness. Choose hope above all things, above what can be seen, above what cannot be seen. Tell them to stand every morning to thank and praise the Lord and also to do the same thing in the evening. Praise and give thanks.

Therefore, since we have been justified through faith, we have peace with God through our Lord Jesus Christ, through whom we have gained access by faith into this grace in which we now stand and we rejoice in the hope of the glory of God.

—Romans 5:1–2

February 22

Tend to your heart. Make sure it is soft, pliable, and receptive to My Word. Like the soil of the garden is prepared for the seed, so too prepare your heart for My Word. Trust Me in all things. Do not doubt My goodness. Allow Me to be strong when you feel weak. Open up your heart of worship to Me. There is no greater love than this.

Come to me, all you who are weary and burdened, and I will give you rest. Take my yoke upon you and learn from me, for I am gentle and humble in heart, and you will find rest for your souls. For my yoke is easy and my burden is light.

—Matthew 11:28–30

February 23

The only leaders qualified to lead are those who have learned to serve. I did not come to be served; I came to serve. It's important that your heart is geared to serve, to pour out your life for others. Go beyond the feelings and give to others because you do it out of love for Me. I run to and fro to show Myself strong on behalf of those whose hearts are loyal to Me. Keep this desire in your people's hearts forever, and keep their hearts loyal to Me.

> For the eyes of the LORD range throughout the earth to strengthen those whose hearts are fully committed to him.
>
> —2 Chronicles 16:9

February 24

Experience My love, walk in My love, hold onto My love. There is nothing greater than love. My love will draw others to you. Share the love I have put in your heart—share your love at all times. Give it away freely. Love covers, lifts up, heals, comforts, encourages. There is so much to My love that cannot be experienced in the world. Spend time allowing Me to fill you up with love so you can be a continuous fountain of life to others.

> The teaching of the wise is a fountain of life, turning a man from the snares of death.
>
> —Proverbs 13:14

February 25

I AM the answer to the world. I AM in the process of changing this world in a very dramatic way. Keep your eyes and ears open and make sure to be obedient to everything I ask of you. Opportunities are in your midst; look for them. Tell the world about Me. Give them the good news. Don't delay. Be broken bread and poured out wine in My hands for the sake of others. Time is short. Speak truth with boldness and courage. There is no time to waste—go forth.

> For the bread of God is he who comes down from heaven and gives life to the world.
>
> —John 6:33

February 26

Worship Me alone. Take a look at your life to find what comes before Me. Is it work, is it children, or is it your spouse? Put no other gods before Me. Put nothing before Me that you think will bring you fulfillment. I AM the only One who can fulfill you and meet your daily needs. Let your faith be in Me alone. I AM a jealous God and want all of you.

> You shall have no other gods before me.
>
> —Exodus 20:3

February 27

Where is your heart regarding those who are wounded, broken, troubled, or lost? Have compassion and mercy on them. Pour out your life and take time to give away compassion and mercy. Dwell on all I have done for you and do not keep it for yourself. Think about the times when you doubted, when you walked away, when you felt lost and hopeless. Think about what I have done for you. Remember when you had to learn to surrender and abandon yourself to Me? Be comforted by the mercy and compassion I have for you and extend it to others. Do not hold back.

> For the LORD comforts his people and will have compassion on his afflicted ones.
> —Isaiah 49:13

February 28

Be a giver. Be generous with your time, your money, and your gifts. It's better to give than receive. Have a giving and serving heart. Be a sharp, keen instrument of righteousness to do good works. Walk in obedience; listen to My promptings of what to do and where to go. I will direct your path. I can trust you with the small things and I can trust you with the large things too. There are many blessings that are yours for the asking. Ask.

Righteousness goes before him and prepares the way for his steps.

—Psalm 85:13

February 29

The giftings you have are not the same as anyone else's. They are unique to you, but you are to work with others. What you have, others need. What you need, others have. That's the way My kingdom works. Nothing is impossible for Me, and I AM the One who gives the gifts as I please. Work together. You have different gifts, according to the grace given to you. Remember, I AM in the midst of your coming and going. Walk in love, walk in humility, walk in faith.

There are different kinds of gifts, but the same Spirit. There are different kinds of service, but the same LORD. There are different kinds of working, but the same God works all of them in all men.

—1 Corinthians 12:4–6

MARCH

March 1

I WILL GIVE you all the strength you need today. Do not worry about tomorrow, for it will take care of itself. Whatever state you are in, be content. Stop and listen to what I have to say to you today. Remember, the name of the Lord is a strong tower; the righteous run to it and are safe. My words to you will give you peace and direction. You can count on that. I AM made strong in your weakness. Wait for Me; be strong and take heart and wait for Me.

> Be strong and courageous. Do not be afraid or terrified because of them, for the LORD your God goes with you; he will never leave you nor forsake you.
> —Deuteronomy 31:6

March 2

Follow My leading—you won't go wrong or be led astray. Listen to My voice as to when to go and when to rest. There is a time for both. My desire is that you hear My voice and obey. I want to use you as a minister of the gospel, but you must know it is I who speak and not you. Meditate on My Word. Know My ways. Know My thoughts. Know that I speak to you in a very special way. Listen, rest, and then listen again.

> Those who oppose him he must gently instruct, in the hope that God will grant them repentance leading them to a knowledge of the truth, and that they will come to their senses and escape from the trap of the devil, who has taken them captive to do his will.
>
> —2 Timothy 2:25–26

March 3

God's love is the most important principle I can teach you. To love all, be good to all, be kind to all. Let them see the love in your heart. The banner over you is love. Be strong, be confident that I AM your God and I will be there for you. The love of God is My nature, for everything comes from God alone. Everything lives by His power and everything is for His glory. Sit under the shelter of love and be comforted by it. My love endures forever. It is My covenant with the world.

O Lord, God of Israel, there is no God like you in heaven or on earth—you who keep your covenant of love with your servants who continue wholeheartedly in your way.

—2 Chronicles 6:14

March 4

I AM with you in your afflictions. Count it all joy. There is a quality of endurance I AM building in you. Do not despair, and look up to Me. My strength is made perfect in your weakness. Commit your ways to Me, trust and lean on Me. Be still and rest. Stay in prayer and stay faithful.

Be joyful in hope, patient in affliction, faithful in prayer. Share with God's people who are in need.

—Romans 12:12–13

March 5

Put yourself in My hands. My kingdom is righteousness, peace, and joy in the Holy Ghost. Know that when you pray, I listen. Let My will be done in your life, not your own will. Do not fear anything. Stay on track; stay in the place I have told you to stay. Do not get distracted or pulled into other things that will drain you physically, mentally, emotionally, or spiritually. Make sure the oil is flowing into your life at all times.

We must go through many hardships to enter the kingdom of God.

—Acts 14:22

March 6

Put on the new man, put off the old self. Enjoy your life and do not waste precious moments. Let My light shine through you, and let your light shine to a world that is hurting. Have fun, laugh, smell the flowers, and make note of My beauty surrounding you and that which is in you. You are My workmanship, My masterpiece. Oh, if you could just grasp My love for you. Oh, if you would just realize how much I desire you to be a part of My life. Know that these words are true.

For we are God's workmanship, created in Christ Jesus to do good works, which God prepared in advance for us to do.

—Ephesians 2:10

March 7

I AM faithful to complete that which I started. I AM a good God and will bring good out of everything. Trust Me in this. I AM your friend. Nothing can separate you from My love. My love cannot be earned. Do not toil, do not worry, do not question. Your life is in My hands and nothing is impossible for Me.

For I am convinced that neither death nor life, neither angels nor demons, neither the present nor the future, nor any powers, neither height nor depth, nor anything else in all creation, will be able to separate us from the love of God that is in Christ Jesus our LORD.

—Romans 8:38–39

March 8

I have called you; I have anointed you to tell the good news. The good news is that I AM reaching out to the world and I AM looking for a response. You are bold, courageous, and wise. The good news you share is not to bring condemnation but to bring conviction to hearts that have fallen away from Me. Do not consider how they might reject you or even despise you. They despised Me first. Shake off any concern. Those who have ears to hear will hear.

These, then, are the things you should teach. Encourage and rebuke with all authority. Do not let anyone despise you.

—Titus 2:15

March 9

Be ambitious for Me but be cautious about your motives. Always come with a heart to serve. Surrender all you have and all you are to Me. I will then equip you to do all I require of you. I will give you that specific word, that specific knowledge, that specific truth that will set many free. Your heart must always be pure and your mind set on Me. You must have the mind of Christ—that which I give you. You cannot see from your perspective but only from Mine. Trust in My leading.

> Create in me a pure heart, O God, and renew a steadfast spirit within me. Do not cast me from your presence or take your Holy Spirit from me.
> —Psalm 51:10–11

March 10

What others think is of no concern when it comes to the things I have asked you to do. Do not compare yourself to others—that is not wise. Your life is in My hands. Let My glory shine in your everyday activities. I AM more concerned about who you are than what you do. Let My glory fill the earth and let My presence be known. Stay on course—do not swerve to the left or to the right. Walk the narrow road.

But everyone knows that you stand loyal and true. This makes me very happy. I want you always to remain very clear about what is right and to stay innocent of any wrong.

—Romans 16:19 TLB

March 11

Look to Me and be not ashamed. Walk in the radiance of My glory. Taste and see that I AM good—trust in Me. I AM your refuge from troubles, concerns, fears, and any other burdens. I AM here for you always—during the storms, during the dark hours, in the midst of it all. Come into My presence. Call out My name. I hear the faintest call. Take time to be with Me during the day. You can be assured that I care about you and all your needs.

Those who look to him are radiant; their faces are never covered with shame. This poor man called, and the LORD heard him; he saved him out of all his troubles.

—Psalm 34:5–6

March 12

Live by your faith—do not be self-sufficient or proud but live dependent on your faith. Do not live by the world's standards but live with eternity in your heart. Surrender your life to Me—be My disciple. Your sufficiency is in Me. Lay down your desires and seek only those things I have placed on your heart. You question and you doubt, but know that no matter what is going on, I AM looking at it from an eternal perspective, not a temporal perspective.

> The man who loves his life will lose it, while the man who hates his life in this world will keep it for eternal life. Whoever serves me must follow me; and where I am, my servant also will be. My Father will honor the one who serves me.
>
> —John 12:25–26

March 13

Listen to My voice, open your eyes to see, hear the sounds of a lost world; the harvest is now. The world is lost and lonely, they need a Savior—go and tell someone the good news today. Proclaim Jesus Christ. There is assurance of victory and peace for those who will trust in Me.

> We proclaim to you what we have seen and heard, so that you also may have fellowship with us. And our fellowship is with the Father and with his Son, Jesus Christ.
>
> —1 John 1:3

March 14

One act of disobedience can change the course of your life. Think again before choosing your way over God's will. I have been leading and guiding you through each step of obedience. Blessings have followed each step. Rejoice in this way of obedience. Yielding to Me will break any bondage of slavery. Blessings are yours for the asking—listen for your marching orders and obey every prompting.

> In everything that he undertook in the service of God's temple and in obedience to the law and the commands, he sought his God and worked wholeheartedly. And so he prospered.
> —2 Chronicles 31:21

March 15

What's the condition of your heart today? Have you taken time to listen to it? Many issues you deal with come from the heart. What burdens are you carrying around? Remember, My yoke is easy and My burden is light. Give your burdens to Me. Trust Me, trust My Word. Do not harden your heart or carry things that are not yours to carry.

> All a man's ways seem right to him, but the LORD weighs the heart. To do what is right and just is more acceptable to the LORD than sacrifice.
> —Proverbs 21:2–3

March 16

Seek and you will find. Be diligent in pursuing a relationship with Me. Spend time finding out more about Me. My love for you is so great. I desire to spend more time with you. I AM right here by your side—draw near to Me. Let Me hold you, comfort you, speak to you. I AM your source of life.

> I love those who love me, and those who seek me find me.
>
> —Proverbs 8:17

March 17

Every day of your life is precious—every moment is a memory to hold on to. Whatever the struggle, whatever the trial, your life is in My hands. This life is temporary compared to your eternal life. Walk in joy, walk with confidence, and walk in your God-given authority. Pray often; ask and wait. Let Me renew your strength when you are weak.

> You have made known to me the ways of life; You will make me full of joy in Your presence.
>
> —Acts 2:28 NKJV

March 18

A life dependent only on Me—what does that really mean? You must surrender totally everything, everyone, every circumstance, every thought, and every action to Me. Rely on all that I AM and all that I will BE in your time of need. Do not dwell on the past or even yesterday; let it go. It's a new day—only today with Me is all that matters. Know and be assured of My great love for you. Do not doubt. Surrender all.

> And so, dear brothers, I plead with you to give your bodies to God. Let them be a living sacrifice, holy—the kind he can accept. When you think of what he has done for you, is this too much to ask?
> —Romans 12:1 TLB

March 19

The road is narrow. At times you can't even see it. Maybe it's rocky, maybe it's hard, and maybe it's full of obstacles, here, there, and everywhere. Nonetheless, it's the road I AM asking you to walk. I know you are weary. I know it's not fun and easy, but My ways and My plans are not always what you think they should be. As a child puts his trust in a loving, nurturing parent, trust Me because I AM your Abba Father who loves you dearly.

Enter through the narrow gate. For wide is the gate and broad is the road that leads to destruction, and many enter through it. But small is the gate and narrow the road that leads to life, and only a few find it.
—Matthew 7:13–14

March 20

Just as the birds sing to begin a fresh morning, just as the wind blows so softly and quietly, just as the flowers bloom and give their scent and color as beauty, so too you are part of the plan. There is nothing that happens in this world on which I didn't already put My signature, including you. Rest in the stillness of it all. Look, hear, feel, and know My presence. Enjoy My creation and handiwork—you are a part of My plan!

For those God foreknew he also predestined to be conformed to the likeness of his Son, that he might be the firstborn among many brothers. And those he predestined, he also called; those he called, he also justified; those he justified, he also glorified.
—Romans 8:29–30

March 21

Lay down your burdens. I will carry you. Their weight is too much for you. They are Mine to carry, not yours. Be My disciple and give Me everything because you are Mine and I call you friend. It is the shout of faith that declares and claims victory. Walk in total and complete faith in who I AM and who I can be for you in all of life's circumstances.

> Take my yoke upon you and learn from me, for I am gentle and humble in heart, and you will find rest for your souls. For my yoke is easy and my burden is light.
>
> —Matthew 11:29–30

March 22

It's the stillness, the waiting, the quietness that can revive and restore your soul. Circumstances in your life will always want your attention and focus, but it is in the stillness of the moment when you will know My presence. Take time to sit before Me without worrying what the world says. It's not a waste of your time. My ability to guide and direct you is dependent on whether you hear My voice. Unfortunately, circumstances and situations can be such a distraction that they cloud your ability to hear. Sit, wait, listen, hear, and obey. You can trust Me to know what is the very best for you. I'm waiting for you.

> The LORD is good to those whose hope is in him, to the one who seeks him; it is good to wait quietly for the salvation of the LORD.
>
> —Lamentations 3:25–26

March 23

Where the Spirit of the Lord is, there is liberty. What liberty, what freedom are you specifically asking for? What is your desire? Where do you feel that you need more of Me and less of you? Do you ask these questions? Have you considered the cross and all that it means for you? My shed blood, My love, My sacrifice were for you! Focusing on Me and less on you or your circumstance will bring that liberty in your life. Have you sought Me today? What concerns you today? I AM waiting for your call, your request, and your petition.

> Now the LORD is the Spirit, and where the Spirit of the LORD is, there is freedom.
> —2 Corinthians 3:17

March 24

As a river flows without interruption, so are the days of your life to flow. The river follows the path outlined for it and doesn't question its destiny. There are things in your life that have caused logjams in your river. Today, I want you to know that I AM in the process of removing those jams. I want you to trust and know that as you rest and trust in the process, your river will flow with ease. The river of Life, the river of Peace, the river of Joy, the river of Grace, the river of Mercy, and the river of God are at the source of your existence and your day-to-day walk. Rejoice and be glad, for this is the day the Lord has made—and it's especially planned for you.

Then the angel showed me the river of the water of life, as clear as crystal, flowing from the throne of God and of the Lamb down the middle of the great street of the city.

—Revelation 22:1–2

March 25

Just as trees, plants, and flowers grow naturally, so shall you mature in your spiritual growth. Just as a parent helps a child grow, take small steps, and begin to walk and talk in a new way, so must you surround yourself with those who can assist in your spiritual growth. It's always a process of growth and not a one-time event. Don't despair and don't get frustrated. A solid root system takes time to grow before the fruit can reveal itself. Be patient but yet passionate about how I want to grow you up.

By their fruit you will recognize them. Do people pick grapes from thornbushes, or figs from thistles? Likewise every good tree bears good fruit, but a bad tree bears bad fruit. A good tree cannot bear bad fruit, and a bad tree cannot bear good fruit. Every tree that does not bear good fruit is cut down and thrown into the fire. Thus, by their fruit you will recognize them.

—Matthew 7:16–20

March 26

I AM your God—faithful and true to My promises. The enemy has attempted to kill, steal, and destroy all I have for you. Remember, he has been defeated and has no power except the power you give him. Know that My ways, My thoughts, and My love for you outweigh everything. There is nothing that can separate you from My love. I AM love, and everything you are about is love. Hold it close in your heart and never doubt it.

> For I am convinced that neither death nor life, neither angels nor demons, neither the present nor the future, nor any powers, neither height nor depth, nor anything else in all creation, will be able to separate us from the love of God that is in Christ Jesus our LORD.
>
> —Romans 8:38–39

March 27

What do you think about? What do you ponder in your heart? What is your mind focused on? Know that you can tap into My presence and My Spirit every moment of the day. I died so you would have life in all things. Don't be deceived by impure thoughts. Don't be discouraged by your circumstances. Don't let your mind wander on anything that is not My character, nature, or Word. Rejoice, I say, rejoice. Praise and thank Me for all things. Be grateful!

Finally, brothers, whatever is true, whatever is noble, whatever is right, whatever is pure, whatever is lovely, whatever is admirable—if anything is excellent or praiseworthy—think about such things.

—Philippians 4:8

March 28

Come to Me as a child, knowing I AM your Father. A Father who loves and comforts you. A Father who will be with you in the hard struggles of life. I AM also a Father who loves you enough to bring correction and discipline in your life so you can experience the fullness of all I have for you. Don't run from correction; let Me show you the way. Keep your wonder and playfulness before Me and I will always be the One with whom you can be real. Don't look to Me from your natural eyes but look to Me from your heart. My love and heart are open to you, My child, anytime, anywhere you call out My name. Be assured of that.

Apply your heart to instruction and your ears to words of knowledge.

—Proverbs 23:12

March 29

Let Me consume you—every part of your life. Lay your burdens and desires at the cross. Let your passion and fire burn brightly and with fervor for My glory. Draw close to Me because I AM your hiding place. When you are weak, I AM strong. Let Me cleanse you, wash over you, and make you white as snow through the power of My blood. My mercies are great and new every day.

> But because of his great love for us, God, who is rich in mercy, made us alive with Christ even when we were dead in transgressions—it is by grace you have been saved.
>
> —Ephesians 2:4–5

March 30

My Spirit is alive and well. Walk in the Spirit and not in the flesh. Use all the power available to you. Stay connected to the power source. Be of good cheer, be of great hope, and know that all things—I mean all things—are possible through Me. Oh, if you could know how much it means to Me that you are My child and I love you so dearly. I thought of you on the cross, and although I experienced great pain and suffering, know that it was My pleasure to set you free from bondage. I conquered it all. Never underestimate the power of My love!

The Spirit gives life; the flesh counts for nothing. The
words I have spoken to you are spirit and they are life.

—John 6:63

March 31

Do not expect love, gratitude, or acknowledgment
from any source. I will give you all necessary rewards.
As you serve Me, you have your reward. It's important
for you to be ready for any battle. Don't think you will
be ready if confronted with a crisis. It is the crisis that
will build something within you—it will reveal what you
are really made of. My training for you is hidden as you
worship Me. My training ground will come from those
hurtful times, those times where you feel abandoned
and lonely, those times when you lose loved ones, those
times when all you can do is get up for the day, those
times that no one even notices that you are alive. Always
remember, you are alive in Me!

But when you pray, go into your room, close the
door and pray to your Father, who is unseen. Then
your Father, who sees what is done in secret, will
reward you.

—Matthew 6:6

APRIL

April 1

WHEN YOU YIELD to temptation, you have made lust your god. I will not save you from temptations, but I will sustain you in the midst of them. I will instruct you, I will teach you, I will give you strength when you feel weak. At times your flesh is stronger and will fight for control. Crucify it, crucify it. Rise up to be the spiritual man revealed in My book—one who can deny the things of the world for the sake of having Me.

> No temptation has seized you except what is common to man. And God is faithful; he will not let you be tempted beyond what you can bear. But when you are tempted, he will also provide a way out so that you can stand up under it.
>
> —1 Corinthians 10:13

April 2

My sheep know My voice. I AM the Great Shepherd to lead and guide you through all seasons of your life. I stand at the gate and protect you from the enemy. Oh, that you would recognize Me in a way that you would trust My leading. I won't lead you astray. You are a part of My sheepfold and I know you personally. When you struggle, I AM there. When you cry and call out to Me, I hear you. When you have needs, I AM here to provide what you need. Don't doubt that I care for you. Just trust in My leading.

> The LORD is my shepherd, I shall not be in want. He makes me lie down in green pastures, he leads me beside quiet waters, he restores my soul.
>
> —Psalm 23:1–2

April 3

You must be still and know that I AM. Your refuge must always be My fortress, your all in all, your front line of defense, your safe place, your covering by My love. Don't keep turning your heart back to Egypt—trust Me that I have delivered you and set you free. I AM your source of strength whenever you need it. Egypt is deceiving and a place of dryness and death. Cross over your Jordan and stay where I have you. Rest your soul in My promises, your future in a land of milk and honey. Come and stay awhile. Come and walk in obedience.

But our fathers refused to obey him. Instead, they rejected him and in their hearts turned back to Egypt.

—Acts 7:39

April 4

My child, My desire is for us to come close and even closer as you live your life. I know there are trials and tribulations with which you are struggling, but know I AM here to carry the burdens. Keep your eyes and your heart focused on Me. Do not doubt or grow faint. My power and My love are available to you to guide and direct. Ask often for wisdom and I will give it to you. Don't listen to the adversary, but listen to the truth of what I say. Let these times mold and shape you. Learn to flow from a place of rest.

Be self-controlled and alert. Your enemy the devil prowls around like a roaring lion looking for someone to devour. Resist him, standing firm in the faith.

—1 Peter 5:8–9

April 5

Turn your eyes upon Me. Look to Me for all you need. I AM your provider in all things. Trust in Me, My Word, and My heart for you. As a father looks out for his child, I too look after you. There is so much you don't understand about My love and My power to save. You can count on Me to pull you through this wilderness time. No, I haven't left you; no, I haven't forgotten about what you need. I AM working out all details of your life. Just yield your will to My will, and trust. Turn your eyes to Me and focus on My faithfulness and goodness as a Father who loves you more than you will ever know. Rest your soul and experience My peace during financial troubles. Keep your faith strong and know that I AM all you need.

> But the Helper, the Holy Spirit, whom the Father will send in My name, He will teach you all things, and bring to your remembrance all things that I said to you. Peace I leave with you, My peace I give to you; not as the world gives do I give to you. Let not your heart be troubled, neither let it be afraid.
> —John 14:26–27 NKJV

April 6

Come into My presence, where there is fullness of joy. Come and be still. Come to rest. Come to receive. Take time today to hear My voice, and let Me pour out My refreshing on you. I AM so delighted to spend time with you today. As you let Me embrace you, My heart becomes full and alive. Many of My children run to and fro to seek My presence, but the truth is, they don't stop long enough to receive Me. But not with you. You have known and experienced the secret place. Come, My precious one, let's talk—let's be together.

Whoever has my commands and obeys them, he is the one who loves me. He who loves me will be loved by my Father, and I too will love him and show myself to him.

—John 14:21

April 7

You are my ambassador to show the world My love. People are watching you and how you love, not so much what you do. Your light must shine for all to see and not be put under a bushel. The world needs someone like you—someone who will love them. They have been wounded by the world and are crying out for more love. Love lives in you more than you know. It is My perfect love that casts out all fear. It is the kind of love that many have never experienced. Be My hands, be My feet, be someone others can trust. If they don't know Me personally, they will know Me and experience Me through you. The challenge is, will you be used?

You are the light of the world. A city on a hill cannot be hidden. Neither do people light a lamp and put it under a bowl. Instead they put it on its stand, and it gives light to everyone in the house. In the same way, let your light shine before men, that they may see your good deeds and praise your Father in heaven.

—Matthew 5:14–16

April 8

There are traps the enemy is putting in your walk that are attempting to slow you down or even stop you from My purposes and destiny for you. These are old traps that just seem to reoccur and reoccur and have set up patterns in your life that stop your progress. Go back to where this trap first had an impact in your life and I will reveal the root cause and bring healing. If the trap or traps are not removed, they will continue to hinder what I have for you. My power is much greater than any trap the enemy sets, but you must seek Me to reveal the truth. My truth will set you free. The enemy has no power other than what you have given him, so know, My child, I have conquered the enemy through My death on the cross so you can walk in freedom. It's a freedom you have never known, and it's yours for the asking. Be still, search your heart, and let Me reveal the plan and strategy where the enemy first set his trap.

> See to it that no one misses the grace of God and that no bitter root grows up to cause trouble and defile many.
>
> —Hebrews 12:15

April 9

Sing a new song. It's a new day, it's a new way, and it's a new song. Sing a song in your heart. Let it rise up and let it set you free. Sing praises to My name. Praise will break open new pathways to freedom. When all else fails, praise. Come out of your cave, see the light, and sing praises of what I have done for you. There is no other day than today. Let your spirit rise above your soul and sing a new song! Trust Me like no other time. Your enemies will fall at My name—let Me inhabit the praises of My people!

Praise the LORD. Sing to the LORD a new song, his praise in the assembly of the saints.
—Psalm 149:1

April 10

Settle down and know that I AM your provider, guide, teacher, and best friend. You have struggled to love, to give, to trust, and to be in relationship with others. Rest and know My heart for you. It is one of righteousness, peace, and joy. What the enemy means for evil, I will turn to good. The promises I have spoken to you and the words you have heard Me say are true; you do hear Me clearly. I love your heart to obey, knowing that faith without works is dead. Walk into this next season with courage.

Be on your guard; stand firm in the faith; be men of courage; be strong. Do everything in love.
—1 Corinthians 16:13–14

April 11

My heart is for you, My heart is in you, and My heart is your resource to a dark and dying world. My sword—My Word—is your weapon. You are a mighty warrior and fully equipped for battle. You lack nothing. Don't look back to the past but keep your eyes, ears, and heart open for opportunities. You are more than a conqueror in Christ.

> For the word of God is living and active. Sharper than any double-edged sword, it penetrates even to dividing soul and spirit, joints and marrow; it judges the thoughts and attitudes of the heart.
>
> —Hebrews 4:12

April 12

I hear your voice and I see your tears. Not one day goes by that My arms don't hold you tight, even in the midst of pain and suffering. Where you feel you are tired and weary, even in a parched and dry land, I AM your living water—you will never thirst. You are sheltered and secure in My presence. I AM a sanctuary for you to experience My power and glory. All I have is yours. Yes, times can be hard and difficult—I know, I know. Remember, I AM only a heartbeat away; a word, a breath, a tear away. Call on Me. Do not delay!

O God, you are my God, earnestly I seek you; my soul thirsts for you, my body longs for you, in a dry and weary land where there is no water. I have seen you in the sanctuary and beheld your power and your glory. Because your love is better than life, my lips will glorify you. I will praise you as long as I live, and in your name I will lift up my hands. My soul will be satisfied as with the richest of foods; with singing lips my mouth will praise you. On my bed I remember you; I think of you through the watches of the night. Because you are my help, I sing in the shadow of your wings. My soul clings to you; your right hand upholds me.

—Psalm 63:1–8

April 13

Oh, ye of little faith. One bump in the road, one mistake, one unloving action or word throws you off the path. The little things in life can be your biggest obstacles. What is it you are looking for? As much as man, especially those close to you, desires to love and give to you, you trip up on what isn't rather than what is. It's a pattern of behaving and responding that is from the old self, the old ways, and the old path to unhappiness. Make a decision today. Think on those things that are pure loving, life giving, and joyful. Don't lose one minute to the old nature. It does not serve you or them. Love, love, love!

So from now on we regard no one from a worldly point of view. Though we once regarded Christ in this way, we do so no longer. Therefore, if anyone is in Christ, he is a new creation; the old has gone, the new has come!
—2 Corinthians 5:16–17

April 14

Just as the sun rises and breaks the day, so too does My Book of Love open up your way. As you ponder on those who loved and obeyed versus those who were defiant and lukewarm, it is obvious I desire unconditional surrender. Oh, if you could only see your great and glorious future. You wouldn't question or doubt anything. I AM your Rock and your Redeemer, and I will guide you into all truth. Open up your heart and trust Me.

They remembered that God was their Rock, that God Most High was their Redeemer.
—Psalm 78:35

April 15

Do not be alarmed or waver from the circumstances in your daily life. You have heard My voice clearly. What the enemy plans for evil, I will turn to good. The road may seem hard at times, but always leave your burden and come to Me. This is a glorious time in your life and a wonderful gift to Me. Remember, keep Me at the center of all that you do. Keep your eyes on Me alone.

When times are good, be happy; but when times are bad, consider God has made the one as well as the other. Therefore, a man cannot discover anything about his future.

—Ecclesiastes 7:14

April 16

Watch My hand, listen to My heart, see the mighty things I AM about to do in your life. Be expectant and refuse the world's lies. Keep focused on Me and keep on the path I have called you to. It's unlike anything you have experienced. Allow Me to have complete access. You won't be disappointed, because what I have called you to do has nothing to do with success or failure. It's My work. Trust in Me completely. Many will be blessed and set free by your obedience to the call. You are chosen for such a time as this.

The LORD's right hand is lifted high; the LORD's right hand has done mighty things!

—Psalm 118:16

April 17

I AM your sufficiency and your strength when you are weak. In the midst of fog, in those places where you can't see, look around and see that things are changing. My presence is surrounding you and My glory is your rear guard. What would life be without Me? Consider this: I died so you could live. My death on the cross was for your freedom. My strength is yours for the asking. My eyes are yours for the asking; My ears are yours for the asking. I have you in My right hand, safe and secure.

> Then your light will break forth like the dawn, and your healing will quickly appear; then your righteousness will go before you, and the glory of the LORD will be your rear guard. Then you will call, and the LORD will answer; you will cry for help, and he will say: Here am I.
>
> —Isaiah 58:8–9

April 18

How easily and quickly you have forgotten the wonderful deeds I have done for you. Even when I deliver you from Egypt, you soon forget. You then are not patient for My hand to move but choose idols. How quickly you don't believe in the promises that I will care for you. You complain and grumble and eventually disobey Me. Just as Moses in the wilderness begged Me to turn from My anger, so I will remember My covenant with you. My unfailing love will be enough.

> Therefore, say to the Israelites: "I am the LORD, and I will bring you out from under the yoke of the Egyptians. I will free you from being slaves to them, and I will redeem you with an outstretched arm and

with mighty acts of judgment. I will take you as my own people and I will be your God. Then you will know that I am the LORD your God, who brought you out from under the yoke of the Egyptians. And I will bring you to the land I swore with uplifted hand to give to Abraham, to Isaac and to Jacob. I will give it to you as a possession. I am the LORD."

—Exodus 6:6–8

April 19

My heart is open to you today and I desire to be found by you. I know life is busy and chaotic but know that I want to bring a refreshing to you. I AM the source of all peace and rest. I AM the One who can accomplish great things through you. I am calling you to come up higher and deeper in your revelation of My power. Your life is like a constant stream of water that must keep moving so it won't become stagnate. So know that your source is Me and the outflow will benefit others.

> For I will pour water on the thirsty land,
> and streams on the dry ground;
> I will pour out my Spirit on your offspring,
> and my blessing on your descendants.

—Isaiah 44:3 NIV

April 20

Let go of all that concerns you today. Put your life completely in My hands. Do not hold anything back. I want you to have freedom and perfect peace. Give all to Me and know that as the great Potter, I will create a life that is abundantly, exceedingly more than you could ever imagine. It takes trust and it takes a full surrender. Seek Me and I will heal all that binds you or limits you from experiencing My presence. I promise you the best.

> "Go down to the potter's house, and there I will give you my message." [3]So I went down to the potter's house, and I saw him working at the wheel. [4]But the pot he was shaping from the clay was marred in his hands; so the potter formed it into another pot, shaping it as seemed best to him.
>
> —Jeremiah 18:2–4 NIV

April 21

Put no other gods before Me. They will lead you to destruction and disobedience. Stand for what is right and from a place of holiness and humility. Don't be distracted with that which takes you away from Me and My purposes. Just as when Shadrach, Meshach, and Abednego did not compromise the truth about their God, do not compromise what I have been for you. Just as they were thrown in the fiery furnace, came out unharmed, and didn't even smell like smoke, I have and will continue to lift you out of your fiery trials. You will not be singed or even smell like smoke. So choose Me and My ways, always knowing I AM your God.

Shadrach, Meshach and Abednego replied to the king, "O Nebuchadnezzar, we do not need to defend ourselves before you in this matter. If we are thrown into the blazing furnace, the God we serve is able to save us from it, and he will rescue us from your hand, O king. But even if he does not, we want you to know, O king, that we will not serve your gods or worship the image of gold you have set up."

—Daniel 3:16–18

April 22

The enemy of your soul is the biggest obstacle in your daily life, especially your mind. Forgive and forget those who have hurt you. It's not wise or healthy to hold on to those hurts. I AM your Healer and Comforter, so bring all your concerns to Me. I know there are times when you feel lonely, abandoned, and rejected, but know this, My child, I AM here and will never abandon or reject you. Come and sit awhile with Me. I will wash away all your tears. I'm waiting....

> The Sovereign LORD will wipe away the tears from all faces; he will remove the disgrace of his people from all the earth. The LORD has spoken.
> —Isaiah 25:8

April 23

My child, yes, I have been with you ever since you were a small child. My banner over you is love. My love for you is unending and immeasurable. You can't really imagine the width and depth of My love because it is so expansive and it is all encompassing. Just as your heart beats and lifeblood flows through your body, soul, and spirit, My heart beats for you in the same way. My desires, My dreams, and My promises have been instilled in and around you, which will bring much life. You have the incorruptible seed of Me in you so there never will be failure. Much fruitfulness will come from that seed. Never doubt My love, plans, or purposes. Rest, knowing that all that concerns you today I already have worked out. My question for you: Will you step out and trust Me?

> Having been born again, not of corruptible seed but incorruptible, through the word of God which lives and abides forever, because "All flesh is as grass, and all the glory of man as the flower of the grass. The grass withers, and its flower falls away, But the word of the LORD endures forever."
>
> —1 Peter 1:23–25 NKJV

April 24

There are no other footsteps in which you have to walk. You are uniquely created and you have all that you need. Others' footsteps may be too small or may be too big. Remember, when there is only one set of footsteps, that is when I AM carrying you. Only walk where I tell you to walk, and know that the path I have for you is secure and strong. Yes, there might be obstacles along the way, but keep your eyes focused on Me and on the path I have called you to walk. No other can walk your path for you—it's one designed for us to walk.

> Establish my footsteps in Your word, and do not let any iniquity have dominion over me. Redeem me from the oppression of man, that I may keep Your precepts. Make Your face shine upon Your servant, and teach me Your statutes.
>
> —Psalm 119:133–135 NASB

April 25

You are so beautiful to Me. I have My eyes on you and will never take them off of you or your circumstances. I know you have felt lonely, unloved, abandoned, and rejected by those whom I entrusted with your life. But know this, My precious child, I love you and have always loved you with an unfailing love. When you were broken, so was I. When you were afraid, so was I. When you felt no one heard your cries or even cared about your heart, so did I. You see, we have much in common. It was *the* way and the only way to the cross. Remember, when I was being persecuted, I sweat blood—it was My blood for you. My life, resurrected life, is coming from what I did on the cross so it is with you. Never again doubt My purposes in your life. Instead, let Me refill you and refresh you with My power and love for what lies ahead. I AM using you to be an instrument to take dominion and authority over the enemy. Let My love continue to pour out to those in your life. You will never run dry and thirsty—just come to Me for that Living Water!

For since death came through a man, the resurrection of the dead comes also through a man. For as in Adam all die, so in Christ all will be made alive. But each in his own turn: Christ, the firstfruits; then, when he comes, those who belong to him. Then the end will come, when he hands over the kingdom to God the Father after he has destroyed all dominion, authority and power. For he must reign until he has put all his enemies under his feet.

—1 Corinthians 15:21–25

April 26

I love you. I know you are going through hurts, but I AM the only One on whom you need to depend. Your faith has made you well. When you are weak, then I AM strong. I hear your cries, I see your pain, and I AM here to take them away from you. Past memories are gone; you are forgiven. I forget so shall you forget. You are such a precious child to Me and I have grand plans for you. I AM refining you into fine gold. Give all your burdens to Me. I can carry them. Look to Me always; seek My face.

> And I will bring the third part through the fire, refine them as silver is refined, and test them as gold is tested. They will call on My name, and I will answer them; I will say, "They are My people," and they will say, "The Lord is my God."
> —Zechariah 13:9 NASB

April 27

My patience, My love, My mercy, My grace, and My goodness will follow you all the days of your life. Come and be with Me. Let Me comfort you, encourage you, and direct your steps today. Do not be concerned about those who do evil around you. I AM your sanctuary and I will hide you in a place where those who desire to hurt you cannot reach you. Be confident of My love for you and stand tall, knowing I AM with you.

He who dwells in the shelter of the Most High will rest in the shadow of the Almighty. I will say of the LORD, "He is my refuge and my fortress, my God, in whom I trust."

—Psalm 91:1–2

April 28

Be still and know that I AM God. Your refuge must always be Me—your rock, your defense, and your fortress. Don't run to Egypt for help—it will bring shame and confusion! You will be tempted to look back, to walk back toward what you know. The truth is that you must continue to walk forward, day by day, into your destiny. Egypt is not your destiny—it is only a place of reflection. Know that I AM restoring the years the locust has eaten.

I will repay you for the years the locusts have eaten—the great locust and the young locust, the other locusts and the locust swarm—my great army that I sent among you. You will have plenty to eat, until you are full, and you will praise the name of the LORD your God, who has worked wonders for you; never again will my people be shamed. Then you will know that I am in Israel, that I am the LORD your God, and that there is no other; never again will my people be shamed.

—Joel 2:25–27

April 29

Oh, My dear one, My precious one, I love your heart, your honesty, and your transparency before Me. I see what you say comes from a place of humility and your desire to be more like Me. I hear your struggles, I see your pain, and I know your traps. Some traps were put on you as a child and some you put on yourself. I've heard your repentance. Know you are forgiven and know I remember your sins no more.

> For I will forgive their wickedness and will remember their sins no more.
>
> —Hebrews 8:12

April 30

I AM your friend, your only source of peace. Let Me touch your heart today. Open your eyes to see how almighty and magnificent I AM. I want to be with you just as much as you want to be with Me. There is no one else who can love you as much as I can. Human efforts can't even get close to who I can be for you. It's part of the great plan.

> I am a friend to all who fear you, to all who follow your precepts. The earth is filled with your love, O LORD; teach me your decrees.
>
> —Psalm 119:63–64

MAY

May 1

WHAT DOES YOUR face say about you? What does your heart reveal? There are times when you have felt alone and abandoned, especially by those close to you. Even when you thought they were there to walk with you through anything, you looked around and saw no one. It has caused you great pain and heartache. I have experienced the same thing. Your face can say many things. What do you want the world to know about you and your life with Me? I heal the brokenhearted and bind up their wounds. Your heart has been broken over the years, but remember, out of the issues of the heart, your mouth speaks. Let Me bring healing and wholeness to you so your face and your heart speak of My great love for you!

May the words of my mouth and the meditation of my heart be pleasing in your sight, O LORD, my Rock and my Redeemer.

—Psalm 19:14

May 2

Let go and enjoy the life you have. Cast your cares upon Me. Embrace and enjoy the life I have given you. You are grafted into Me, in the life-giving Vine. Abide in that love. I want you to bear much fruit—not just fruit, but fruit that is long lasting and rich. When it comes to pruning and things are being cut away, know that this has to happen so you will bear much more fruit. All of My children have to walk through the pruning process so they can be strong and built up in Me. Do not pull away from the Vine when the pruning begins. Stay close to Me and trust that I have your future in My hands.

I am the true vine, and my Father is the gardener. He cuts off every branch in me that bears no fruit, while every branch that does bear fruit he prunes so that it will be even more fruitful. You are already clean because of the word I have spoken to you. Remain in me, and I will remain in you. No branch can bear fruit by itself; it must remain in the vine. Neither can you bear fruit unless you remain in me.

—John 15:1–4

May 3

Being rich is not a matter of having things or getting your way. Being rich is knowing and believing God's Word in your life and in your circumstances. I AM your provider and I know exactly what you need when you need it. Trust Me in the small things as well as the big things. Do not get disappointed or dismayed if things don't turn out the way you thought they would today. At the end of the day, take a deep breath and know that your life is in My hands, so be thankful. Just as a father wants to give his children gifts and see the joy on their faces, so too I want to bless you. Trust in Me.

> You will be made rich in every way so that you can be generous on every occasion, and through us your generosity will result in thanksgiving to God.
> —2 Corinthians 9:11

May 4

I want you to fly high as an eagle. You have keen senses to discern your surroundings. You have wisdom where to go. You have all that you need to accomplish your goals and dreams. Eagles represent not only majesty but honor and respect. You have not lacked anything, and you will always be guided by My hand. Fly without hindrances, fly with freedom, fly into the high places, fly with joy, fly with hope, and fly with faith. Follow the wind. Soar with the wind. It doesn't have to take as much energy as you are putting into it. Rest and relax. You were created for rest.

> But those who hope in the LORD will renew their
> strength. They will soar on wings like eagles; they will
> run and not grow weary, they will walk and not be faint.
> —Isaiah 40:31

May 5

I AM longing for you. I AM delighted when you come spend time with Me. When your desire is just for Me and not what I can do for you, My heart leaps with joy. I created you to have relationship with Me. What better place is there than to be in the sweet, loving arms of someone you love? Love that never ends, love that never fails, love that is always available when you call My name. Spend a moment, take a rest, soak in My presence. I will fill you to overflowing, and not only will you be filled but I too will be exuberant with delight.

> Here is my servant whom I have chosen, the one I
> love, in whom I delight; I will put my Spirit on him,
> and he will proclaim justice to the nations.
> —Matthew 12:18

May 6

I AM your Healer and your Comforter. There have been many times when you have looked to others to give you the peace and comfort only I can give. I know you have struggled with your identity and struggled whether you can really trust Me fully or not. I understand. There have been trials and tribulations in your life where you thought I was not there or that I didn't care for you. I understand. There have been disappointments and discouragements along the road where you didn't think I listened. I understand. There has been pain in your heart and you didn't know if you could trust Me completely. I understand. Please don't hold back anymore. I AM available for you, I AM here for you, I do listen, and I do care. Please give Me another opportunity today.

> But I trust in you, O LORD; I say, "You are my God." My times are in your hands; deliver me from my enemies and from those who pursue me. Let your face shine on your servant; save me in your unfailing love.
>
> —Psalm 31:14–16

May 7

You are not a victim. You are strong and victorious in all ways. Don't let self-pity pull you down. All My children are victorious and mighty in Me. I created you that way! There is nothing you can't overcome with My might, My power, and My Spirit. You are not unworthy or valueless in this world. You are very much needed in a world that is dying from self-focus. Just keep your heart, mind, and soul on Me. I will open doors for you to minister to those souls that are lost, but it has to come from a place of victory. Go forth without fear!

So he said to me, "This is the word of the LORD to Zerubbabel: 'Not by might nor by power, but by my Spirit,' says the LORD Almighty."

—Zechariah 4:6

May 8

Real peace comes from Me and nothing else. Issues in your life can be explained more clearly as you spend time with Me. My presence is indispensable in your life. Believe in the impossible. Walk in faith, believing I can meet—in fact, exceed—all you can imagine or hope for. Think abundantly. Don't limit My resources to you because of unbelief. Have faith that I can move mountains. All things are possible with Me.

He did not waver at the promise of God through unbelief, but was strengthened in faith, giving glory to God, and being fully convinced that what He had promised He was also able to perform.

—Romans 4:20–21 NKJV

May 9

Your words can bless or curse. What is coming out of your mouth? Are your words encouraging, are they building up and edifying, or are they negative and discouraging? Words can bring life or they can bring death. I want to work through you to encourage others. Follow My leading—I will prompt you and show you who needs that word. Make sure to sow seeds of love, joy, encouragement, and help to others. Your harvest may not be immediate, but it will be returned to you a hundredfold. Do to others as you would want them to do to you. You won't go wrong. It's imperative that you see from My eyes and not those of man.

> Do not be deceived, God is not mocked; for whatever a man sows, that he will also reap. For he who sows to his flesh will of the flesh reap corruption, but he who sows to the Spirit will of the Spirit reap everlasting life. And let us not grow weary while doing good, for in due season we shall reap if we do not lose heart. Therefore, as we have opportunity, let us do good to all, especially to those who are of the household of faith.
>
> —Galatians 6:7–10 NKJV

May 10

There is nothing I can't change. I can bring you out of every pit you might fall into. I AM here for you in the good times, the bad times, and the times when you feel your world has stopped. My Word is truth to you and it will make you free any time. Draw on My Word for your strength. I want to heal your broken heart and free you from every bondage that stops you in your tracks. Let My banner of love cover you today and every day. Let My joy be evident everywhere you go.

The Spirit of the Sovereign LORD is on me, because the LORD has anointed me to preach good news to the poor. He has sent me to bind up the broken-hearted, to proclaim freedom for the captives and release from darkness for the prisoners, to proclaim the year of the LORD's favor and the day of vengeance of our God, to comfort all who mourn, and provide for those who grieve in Zion—to bestow on them a crown of beauty instead of ashes, the oil of gladness instead of mourning, and a garment of praise instead of a spirit of despair. They will be called oaks of righteousness, a planting of the LORD for the display of his splendor.

—Isaiah 61:1–3

May 11

It's not so much what you say but what you do. Be a gift and a blessing to those around you. A simple smile can be the greatest form of encouragement. Let it come from your heart. Don't be so focused on what you can get but what you can give. Let go of any negativity or discouragement because it will close your eyes to those around you. Lay your burdens at the cross and let Me carry them. Focus on your strengths and not on your weaknesses. My world needs you, your heart, your wisdom, your love, your kindness, and your ways of appreciation for them. Everyone needs a Savior, and I want to use you today to represent Me.

Give, and it will be given to you. A good measure, pressed down, shaken together and running over, will be poured into your lap. For with the measure you use, it will be measured to you.

—Luke 6:38

May 12

I see your heart. My desire for you is to live in peace when your soul is troubled. Peace is My gift to you—not as the world gives, but My peace I give to you. Don't let confusion, turmoil, or outer circumstances rule in your life. God's kingdom is righteousness, peace, and joy. Desire peace above everything and walk in the Spirit and not in your soul. You can't depend on your soul to make decisions for you. Remember, you don't have power if you don't have peace. Let My peace fill in those dry places, those weary places, those painful places, and let it fill you to overflowing. As you walk in more peace, those around you will also walk in more peace.

Peacemakers who sow in peace raise a harvest of righteousness.

—James 3:18

May 13

Never let the sense of your past failures stop you from taking the next right step. Yes, it has been difficult and there have been many mistakes in the past. Put away the past and know that My blood covers all. What is in your heart for today, tomorrow, or the years ahead? Have you asked yourself lately? Do not let your past define your future. Trust Me with all of your heart, soul, and mind. Know that I AM the Redeemer of the years lost and the Repairer of the Breach. Leave all of it in My hands. I love you and have great plans for you that the enemy has attempted to steal from you. Don't go one more day carrying the hurt and baggage of yesterday.

> Those from among you shall build the old waste places; you shall raise up the foundations of many generations; and you shall be called the Repairer of the Breach, the Restorer of Streets to Dwell In.
> —Isaiah 58:12 NKJV

May 14

Rejoice, rejoice, I say, rejoice. Lift your praises to Me. Sing a new song and praise My name. Praise opens up the heavens to you. Praise fills My heart. Praise is a mighty weapon. Be thankful, grateful, and sing praises to My name—the name above all names. Praise Me in the hard places, praise Me in the happy places, praise Me in the difficulties, and praise Me in the joyful times. Praise will lift you out of the pit of despair and put your feet on solid footing. When you live from a heart of praise, believe Me, it will change the way you think, the way you see things, and the way you live. When you look at all the places I have been in your life, you will realize I have done great things for you!

> Sing to him, sing praise to him; tell of all his wonderful acts. Glory in his holy name; let the hearts of those who seek the LORD rejoice. Look to the LORD and his strength; seek his face always.
> —1 Chronicles 16:9–11

May 15

My grace is sufficient for you, so don't live by works. Do the best you can and I will do the rest of what you can't do. Let Me make the changes that need to be made. Sometimes you strive and drive to make things happen that will happen only by My power. The first change that needs to happen is in you to become more Christlike. Change can happen quickly, but most of the time change happens over time. Relax and let Me make the changes I want in you, to prune you of those things that don't bear fruit. Let Me mold and shape you into Christ's image. Surrender to the Potter's wheel and let Me create a beautiful vessel of God. Enjoy this journey and live in the moment with Me.

But now, O LORD, You are our Father, we are the clay, and You our potter; and all of us are the work of Your hand.

—Isaiah 64:8 NASB

May 16

One life is changed by the way you see yourself and by the way you give of yourself. Live with purpose and live in your godly identity. If you are confused as to whom you are, just open My Book and see for yourself how I see you. It's not how the world sees you that is important. It's how you see yourself through My eyes that is important. Let the light within you shine and touch others with whom you come in contact with. I desire to use you as My hands, feet, mouth, and heart to touch a world that is lost. Your confidence comes from Me. Give, give, give.

In the same way, let your light shine before men, that they may see your good deeds and praise your Father in heaven.

—Matthew 5:15–16

May 17

As a child is wrapped in blankets to keep warm and secure, it is My desire to wrap you in My love to keep you safe. Your security, safety, and protection come from Me and under the shadow of My wings. I AM your refuge from events that would want to harm you, confuse you, or even distract you from your purpose and destiny. Take a minute, close your eyes, and see My arms wrapped around you. Just as an eagle can soar high above the storms, you too can soar in high places—way above your circumstances. The life I have planned for you is one of great power and strength, not one of powerlessness and weakness. Let My Spirit flow in and through you. Let My Spirit fill you to overflowing. Let My power touch you and others. Soar without struggle.

> The eternal God is your refuge, and underneath are the everlasting arms. He will drive out your enemy before you, saying, "Destroy him!"
> —Deuteronomy 33:27

May 18

Look forward and do not look back. I have protected you in ways you can't comprehend. I have been your shelter and your refuge. No matter what you have done, I have forgiven you, My child, so receive your forgiveness. Let My love and blood cleanse you and cover you—knowing that love covers a multitude of sins. Release all those things you are holding in your hands. Know I have wept knowing you have carried these burdens—too much for anyone to carry. Please surrender them to Me this day and know in your heart that it is finished—on the cross and once again today, tomorrow, and forever.

He says, "I removed the burden from their shoulders;
their hands were set free from the basket."
—Psalm 81:6

May 19

There are no flaws in you. I like the way I made you. I
AM not intimidated by those areas in you that are lacking
or that are unhealed, because I AM perfectly able to heal
those areas. Where you have looked at yourself and carried
shame, I replace that shame with honor. Where you have
seen yourself as a failure, I replace that failure with success.
Where you have fallen into a pit, My right hand picks you
up and places your feet on a solid rock. There isn't anything
I can't do. Surrender your life, your ways, your thoughts,
and your perceptions of how you see yourself to Me. When
I created you, I created you in My image—therefore, there
are no flaws. Believe this truth and walk in freedom.

So God created man in his own image, in the image of
God he created him; male and female he created them.
—Genesis 1:27

May 20

I AM your Shepherd. I lead and guide you in the
way I think best. Follow My leading. There are times
when you question or doubt the path I have you on,
but know this: I have your best interests in My heart. I

can see the beginning and the end—you see just a part. Times are tough in the world, but be of good cheer because I have overcome the world. What the world says and what the world does is not your reality. Your reality must be kingdom minded—a bigger picture than what you see with your natural eyes. Trust, believe, and walk in faith, for you are in the palm of My hand.

> The works of his hands are faithful and just; all his precepts are trustworthy. They are steadfast for ever and ever, done in faithfulness and uprightness. He provided redemption for his people; he ordained his covenant forever—holy and awesome is his name.
>
> —Psalm 111:7–9

May 21

My child, you are a new creation created as My masterpiece. You are My mouthpiece and a light unto the world. Do not hide under a bushel; do not let your light go out. Keep fanning the flame and walk in authority! A life full of life is a life that can change external circumstances. A life full of light can lead others who might be lost. A life full of My glory can be seen by others who might otherwise reject Me. Never question My purpose and plan in your life and never doubt My specific plans. Seek Me in the morning, seek Me in the afternoon, seek Me in the evening. Seek Me whenever you can.

For you were once darkness, but now you are light
in the LORD. Live as children of light (for the fruit of
the light consists in all goodness, righteousness and
truth) and find out what pleases the LORD.
—Ephesians 5:8–10

May 22

Your disappointments and hurts are not based on
what is going on in your life today. They are rooted
in hurts of the past. I know that when life is good, it
is good; and when life is bad, it feels as if everything
goes bad. Know this, My child: I AM part of both. My
desire is that you spend time with Me today and not
get busy trying to avoid the pain. It will come and it
will go as you talk to Me and let Me touch that place
of woundedness. There are situations and people in
your life that have contributed to where you might be
emotionally today but know this: I AM your Counselor
and your Healer. Trust your heart with Me. I will hold
it with gentleness and love. Let Me restore you to
wholeness—don't delay.

Heal me, O LORD, and I will be healed; save me and
I will be saved, for you are the one I praise.
—Jeremiah 17:14

May 23

Know that there is nothing or no one that can satisfy your soul other than Me. You have looked to others to fill only those places in your heart I can touch. Accept My love to the deepest crevices in your brokenness and let Me pour My oil to overflowing. I know it is your desire to be like Me, to live like Me, and to love like Me. What you have experienced in those painful days is just a view of what I might have suffered in My quest to save you. Think of these words: On Christ the solid rock I stand; all other ground is sinking sand. Stand on the rock.

> He is the Rock, his works are perfect, and all his ways are just. A faithful God who does no wrong, upright and just is he.
>
> —Deuteronomy 32:4

May 24

Rest and enjoy the peace and calmness. It's a place of security and belonging. Anxious thoughts and impure thinking are not the place I would have you stay. Throughout the day, call on My name, Jesus, for your comfort. In the morning, yoke up with Me. In all the minutes and hours of your day, know I AM at your right side. Just as a river is still and calm, a place of serenity and peace in the natural realm, I AM the only One who can give that stillness, calmness, serenity, and peace in the spiritual realm. You cannot see Me with your eyes but you can sense Me in your heart. My child, come and be refreshed whenever you need it.

> I will refresh the weary and satisfy the faint.
> —Jeremiah 31:25

May 25

Stop and smell the roses. Look around and see My handiwork. It's in the rain, it's in the snow, it's in the wind, it's in the songs of the birds, and it's in the crocuses blooming and the squirrels running to and fro. How often have you run here and there and didn't even notice the most simple of My creation? Many want more and more and are never satisfied but never stop to be thankful for what they already have. I have blessed you abundantly and will continue to bless you. Don't try to live on the mountaintop all the time, and know that I AM also in the valley. There is always new growth happening in the valley. Be grateful and thankful at all times.

> In his hand are the depths of the earth, and the mountain peaks belong to him. The sea is his, for he made it, and his hands formed the dry land. Come, let us bow down in worship, let us kneel before the LORD our Maker; for he is our God and we are the people of his pasture, the flock under his care.
> —Psalm 95:4–7

May 26

I AM your friend. Friends can come and go, but know this: I will never leave you. Friendships change from day to day. Our relationship will change from day to day as we spend time together. Some friendships last forever; some friendships last only short periods of time. There is always a jewel in any relationship, so look for the jewel. Divine appointments can happen when you least expect them. Surprise phone calls will come just when you need them. If you aren't quite sure how to be in a friendship, start with Me. Our friendship can be long lasting and we both can experience great joy!

> Dear friend, I pray that you may enjoy good health and that all may go well with you, even as your soul is getting along well. It gave me great joy to have some brothers come and tell about your faithfulness to the truth and how you continue to walk in the truth. I have no greater joy than to hear that my children are walking in the truth.
>
> —3 John 2–4

May 27

Do you need a miracle today? I AM the God of wonder and miracles. Know that My life itself was a life full of wonder and miracles. That same life lives within you. Lift up your prayers to Me, knowing I hear all your prayers. Do not limit what I can do through you for others. There are many who need a miracle today.

My presence living in you and your obedience to Me can be the miracle for someone else today. Be aware of your surroundings, and don't be surprised that the miracle you need might just come through a divine appointment with others. Have faith and believe in this mighty miracle-power working through you.

> Believe me when I say that I am in the Father and the Father is in me; or at least believe on the evidence of the miracles themselves. I tell you the truth, anyone who has faith in me will do what I have been doing. He will do even greater things than these, because I am going to the Father.
>
> —John 14:11–12

May 28

Laugh, laugh, laugh. When was the last time you experienced joy that not only changed you but also infected others around you? Life is short, and before you even know it, it's gone. Laughter is good medicine to your soul, and it is My desire for you that you experience not only pain and sorrow but also joy and happiness. Remember that the joy of the Lord is your strength—strength in ways you don't even understand. Don't let oppression from your circumstances ever steal your joy! Laughter is one of those gifts that will cause the enemy to run.

There is a time for everything, and a season for every activity under heaven … a time to weep and a time to laugh, a time to mourn and a time to dance.

—Ecclesiastes 3:1, 4

May 29

Trials and tribulations, ups and downs, boredom and exuberance—I AM in them all. When the hills become mountains and the trials become overwhelming, I AM in them all. When confusion and doubt enter in, I AM here for you. Life has many facets, and experiencing joy along with sorrow is a part of that overall grand picture and plan. If you feel burdened and oppressed today, release it all to Me. If you are experiencing boredom in your life today, get busy. Don't fall into the trap of escape and miss out on what I have for you. This day is all you have. Remember, there is nothing you can do about yesterday, and worrying about tomorrow won't help. Know that I have the perfect plan: to give you a future and a hope. Trust in that.

"For I know the plans I have for you," declares the LORD, "plans to prosper you and not to harm you, plans to give you hope and a future."

—Jeremiah 29:11

May 30

I know there are times when you feel barren and dry. You look around and see no fruit from your efforts. You pray and see no answers to your prayers. There are times when you feel like giving up and walking away. You know you won't, but yet that is what you feel. I understand that. Many times in My life I saw nothing fruitful coming from My efforts to see people walk in freedom. Today, My heart breaks for those who desire to walk their own way and leave Me behind or hidden away. Each day I would get up and do the work of My Father. That is what I knew to do. Even in the wilderness I knew Living Water would come to refresh Me and fill My heart—Living Water, not stagnant water. Let Me refresh you today.

> I will make rivers flow on barren heights, and springs within the valleys. I will turn the desert into pools of water, and the parched ground into springs.
> —Isaiah 41:18

May 31

See others as I see them. See them as perfect in Me. Do not judge or criticize what you do not understand. There are times when your heart has been hardened not by what others have done but by the way you have perceived their actions. The world knows very well how to compare, judge, criticize, belittle, mock, and condemn others. That is not part of My kingdom nor

My desire for you to live. You have been taught patterns of communicating that are not helping you in your relationships today. Trust Me and rest in Me, knowing that you are safe and protected from harm. You must learn to love as I love, give as I give, and honor as I honor. Life's instructions are in My Book—know them well.

Do not judge and you will not be judged. Do not condemn and you will not be condemned. Forgive, and you will be forgiven. Give and it will be given to you. A good measure, pressed down, shaken together and running over, will be poured into your lap. For with the measure you use, it will be measured to you.
—Luke 6:37–38

JUNE

June 1

IT'S ALL ABOUT progress and not perfection. Keep moving forward and let My Spirit move, guide, and direct you. Many of the expectations you have put on yourself are not from Me at all. My grace is sufficient for you. Grace—great grace. My grace will enable you to do things you thought were impossible. My grace will teach you and give you wisdom. My grace will build you up and not tear you down. My grace is guaranteed and will fill you with peace. There is an abundant provision of My grace for you. Receive it to the fullest—it is a gift. You are not under law, but you are under grace. I have redeemed you from the law so that you can live in grace—My unmerited favor.

This righteousness from God comes through faith in Jesus Christ to all who believe. There is no difference; for all have sinned and fall short of the glory of God, and are justified freely by his grace through the redemption that came by Christ Jesus.

—Romans 3:22–24

June 2

My child, overlook offenses. Overlook those small things that try to make you frustrated or angry. It's easy to let your heart be troubled if you are focusing on impure thoughts. It is the enemy's plan to get you unsettled and focused on others instead of walking in peace and being focused on Me. Offenses can cause division and strife among you. Offenses can hurt those who love you the most. Keep your heart soft and pliable—free from offense. My remedy is always forgiveness, keeping short accounts, and taking the log out of your own eye. Everything you say or do must come from a pure heart.

A man's wisdom gives him patience; it is to his glory to overlook an offense.

—Proverbs 19:11

June 3

Let My music touch your heart and infiltrate your soul. Let My music touch and heal those places in your heart that are hurting. Music and song are life's gifts to enjoy. I created them and I want you to let them penetrate the very places where sadness resides. I want you to know I inhabit the praises of My people, and it is My desire to inhabit your life. Come to Me with thanksgiving and praises in your mouth, expecting the very best. If you stay silent long enough, you can even hear My heart beating for you and making a sweet sound. Always remember to make music to Me and make music in your heart for others.

> Speak to one another with psalms, hymns and spiritual songs. Sing and make music in your heart to the LORD, always giving thanks to God the Father for everything, in the name of our LORD Jesus Christ.
> —Ephesians 5:19–20

June 4

My favor is upon you. My favor opens doors that I want opened for you. I want you to ask for favor wherever you go. Favor is a blessing and a gift that I want to pour out on you as you seek Me. My favor will give you opportunities you never imagined. My favor will rest on you as you walk out day by day. Look for it—expect it. When you look at others who appear to have influence in their lives, or have others following them desiring relationship, know it is My favor.

I will look on you with favor and make you fruitful and increase your numbers, and I will keep my covenant with you. You will still be eating last year's harvest when you will have to move it out to make room for the new. I will put my dwelling place among you, and I will not abhor you. I will walk among you and be your God, and you will be my people.

—Leviticus 26:9–12

June 5

My promises are true and yours for the asking. My promises and covenant with you never can be forsaken. If you read My Word and look for My promises, they are laid out very clearly for a future and for a destiny that is more than you ever expected or desired. Oh, such joy to know that as you walk with Me, day by day, step by step, My light will shine forth on all you need. My promises are "yes" and "amen." Those in the world do not understand what the word *promise* even means. Even before you came to know Me, you were not sure of what it meant. Promise: providential, redeeming, overcoming, magnificent, ideal, sacrificial, eternal. Much more than you ever imagined. Rest and receive the truth of My promises in your life!

And now, LORD, let the promise you have made concerning your servant and his house be established forever. Do as you promised, so that it will be established and that your name will be great forever.

—1 Chronicles 17:23–24

June 6

Stop and reflect. Take a good look at what I have done for you. Look at where you have been, what you have overcome, and where your family and friends have come so far. Focusing on the negative can stop you from seeing the positive and miraculous things in your life—a simple heartbeat, a breath, the ability to walk or run, and the wonders of what you see and hear. Think of these things. There is no other God like Me. Without Me life is hard and hopeless. With Me, life is full of joy—even during the hard times. I never said you would not have trials. My promise to you is that I will be with you as you walk through the valleys. Think, reflect, and stop and be grateful. I AM your refuge, you are held in My arms, and no one or nothing can harm you.

> No one will be able to stand up against you all the days of your life. As I was with Moses, so I will be with you; I will never leave you nor forsake you.
> —Joshua 1:5

June 7

As you walk and admire My handiwork in this world, notice how many times you see the beauty but fail to see the weeds. You don't have the tendency to focus on the weeds in gardens and you don't judge what you see. Your eyes are drawn to the beauty and to the flowers' fragrance. So too it is with Me. When I look at you, I see My image in you—not those places where you see the flaws. My eyes don't even focus on impurities or places where you might lack. I AM always seeing you through My Father's heart and eyes. Yes, there are places in your life that need My healing touch, but that has no impact on the way I see you. Trust and believe the truth, My child.

> But thanks be to God, who always leads us in triumphal procession in Christ and through us spreads everywhere the fragrance of the knowledge of him. For we are to God the aroma of Christ among those who are being saved and those who are perishing.
>
> —2 Corinthians 2:14–15

June 8

Your value is not based on what you do or what happens to you but whose you are. I AM in control of your life and leading you day in and day out. It is not about right and wrong, it's all about living life to its fullest. Remember, as you believe in your heart, you also put expectations on others. If you think you are wrong, you also think others are wrong. Remember, what you sow, you reap. It is a spiritual law. My love and grace are available for you and for others. People in your life want freedom to be who they are, and you want to walk in the freedom of who you are. Have faith that I AM faithful to complete that which I have begun in you and in others.

From the fullness of his grace we have all received one blessing after another. For the law was given through Moses; grace and truth came through Jesus Christ.

—John 1:16–17

June 9

I AM your Helper and Counselor, but not as the world helps or counsels. I came and died for you so you could live free from bondage. I sent the Holy Spirit to you to bring you comfort, to help you discern My ways and thoughts, to be your friend in times of trouble, to counsel, and to teach you. Oh, that you would know Me! Do not be afraid of what I speak to you or show you. There are many things I have yet to reveal to you. I AM surrounding you with the truth, with loving friends, and with experiences that will strengthen and help you grow. Just as a mother and father love, help, and counsel their children, I too am enabling you to walk in ways that will set you on a path of growth. Experience My peace and rest, knowing that all is well.

For to us a child is born, to us a son is given, and the government will be on his shoulders. And he will be called Wonderful Counselor, Mighty God, Everlasting Father, Prince of Peace.

—Isaiah 9:6

June 10

Be bold, be strong, and walk in courage with the full armor of God. Don't fall into the Devil's wiles. Don't get tripped up with old patterns of thinking and believing. Trust in My Word and trust in your ability to walk in that truth. It's the small things of life that can cause you to get off course. My path is narrow. It is a path that can keep you in a place of protection and safety. Put on the whole armor of God as My mighty child of God and know I AM with you. In My kingdom there is no failure. In My kingdom there *is* righteousness, peace, and joy.

> You broaden the path beneath me, so that my ankles do not turn. I pursued my enemies and overtook them; I did not turn back till they were destroyed. I crushed them so that they could not rise; they fell beneath my feet. You armed me with strength for battle; you made my adversaries bow at my feet. You made my enemies turn their backs in flight, and I destroyed my foes.
>
> —Psalm 18:36–40

June 11

I have joy and satisfaction available to you. Satisfaction, fulfillment, contentment, and pleasure are gifts I want to pour out on you. "But," you say, "I know happiness, but I am not sure I know joy. I have had satisfaction in times and places in my life but dissatisfaction in others. I found contentment maybe where I might not have expected it." Remember, as you walk with Me day in and day out, you will have many experiences that will bring you small and big miracles. Be expectant, be looking, and ask and seek Me for what you want. I want to give you the desires of your heart. I AM delighted to give My children what they want.

> His pleasure is not in the strength of the horse, nor his delight in the legs of a man; the LORD delights in those who fear him, who put their hope in his unfailing love.
>
> —Psalm 147:10–11

June 12

What do you think of when you see a hot air balloon? I am sure you stand in awe and watch. Have you considered all it takes for the balloon to be secure and ready to fly? How much air does it take to fill that balloon so it flies with no restriction? What are the necessary winds required to make the balloon go where it is supposed to go? Consider these things as they relate to your life. All things in your life need to be secure so the foundation is strong. My Holy Spirit and My breath need to fill you. Your ears need to be tuned to Me so you hear My specific instructions on where to go and when. So stand and watch in wonder as your life unfolds.

And with that he breathed on them and said,
"Receive the Holy Spirit."

—John 20:22

June 13

As you look around the landscape of My creation,
stop and take a look at the different shapes, colors,
species, and ages. Some trees, bushes, and flowers are
in different stages of growth. Some have shallow roots,
while others have stronger roots. Notice how all of
them get rained on or watered by Me. They all get sun
but in different times of the day and at different levels.
No one or nothing is left out. I thought about it all.
Know that there is not one detail in your life I haven't
thought about. You are not created like any other. You
are unique, and the timing of events and happenings
in your life is just as unique. Do not compare yourself
with anyone or about anything. Trust that I have it all
under control.

We do not dare to classify or compare ourselves with
some who commend themselves. When they measure
themselves by themselves and compare themselves
with themselves, they are not wise.

—2 Corinthians 10:12

June 14

Am I on your mind today? Have you thought about all those times I rescued you from harm? Have you considered how deep and wide My great love is for you? Have you taken the time to remember how much you mean to Me? I know life is busy and schedules are tight, but nothing is greater than our time together. It is life and breath to you. It is joy to Me. When was the last time you stopped and listened to My voice? Did you obey the instructions? Don't let today's small, insignificant issues block My voice. Don't let man's fears stop you from walking in obedience. Oh, if only you really knew and understood My love for you! Nothing would come between us. I love you.

> On my bed I remember you; I think of you through the watches of the night. Because you are my help, I sing in the shadow of your wings. My soul clings to you; your right hand upholds me.
>
> —Psalm 63:6–8

June 15

Man says you are a failure, you will never amount to anything no matter how hard you try, and nothing will ever turn out the way you want it to. That is what the world says, but that is not what My kingdom is about. My Word says you are an overcomer, you are a mighty warrior, and no weapon formed against you will prosper. What do you believe? Is it based on circumstances or is it based on My truth? Life happens and circumstances tend to lead you down the path of deception. Do not believe what the world says; believe what I say about you and your circumstances. I AM the Way, the Truth, and the Life. That's the truth!

> Jesus replied, "The kingdom of God does not come with your careful observation, nor will people say, 'Here it is,' or 'There it is,' because the kingdom of God is within you."
>
> —Luke 17:20–21

June 16

Peace is yours today. Comfort is yours today. Joy is yours today. Love is yours today. My gifts and treasures are yours today. Sight and sound are yours today. A heart full of compassion and sensitivity is yours today. My grace and mercy are yours today. Ask what you will. Seek and you will find Me. My desire is that you have what you need today.

> Let us then approach the throne of grace with confidence, so that we may receive mercy and find grace to help us in our time of need.
>
> —Hebrews 4:16

June 17

Look around and see the people in your life—they aren't necessarily those you know. Take a good look at their faces. Are there smiles or frowns? Listen to what they are saying or maybe what they aren't saying. What do their eyes look like? Are they sad-looking or eyes of joy and anticipation? Pay attention to those in your specific realm on this earth at this very moment in time. They are there because I have given you the ability to see into men's hearts to gain My heart for them. What do they need from you? It could be a smile, a hug, a kind gesture, or a word of encouragement. You are My arms, My legs, and My smile. You might just be the only one today who seemed to care. Ponder these things. Listen to My voice and do what I say. You won't be disappointed and, just think, neither will they!

> She opens her arms to the poor and extends her hands to the needy.
>
> —Proverbs 31:20

June 18

You are an instrument in My hands and I desire to use you. Let Me use you as a sharp instrument to defeat the enemy in others' lives. Lift your prayers up to Me—I hear each one and I make intercession on your behalf. Some of My children do not have because they do not ask. Don't think you are a bother to Me. I so desire your friendship and your willingness to come and place your trust in Me. Some just depend on their own ways, their own thoughts, or others' thoughts. But you have learned to come to Me first because you understand it is not man's wisdom you seek but God's power! I AM all the power you need. I AM the light in every dark place. I AM your shelter when you need comfort, and I AM your Shepherd to watch over you.

> If a man cleanses himself from the latter, he will be an instrument for noble purposes, made holy, useful to the Master and prepared to do any good work.
> —2 Timothy 2:21

June 19

I AM the God of freedom. I AM your freedom fighter. I execute judgment on the enemy. Your life is one of freedom in which I died so you would walk unencumbered. What is holding you back? I have water for you to drink, food to nourish and strengthen your whole being, wisdom and counsel for you to walk in, friendship for you at all times, favor and blessings in all you do, and liberty in all aspects of your life. What else do you need? I died so you could walk in total freedom, so rejoice, I say, rejoice. Your joy and happiness are in Me and Me alone.

> Blessed is he whose help is the God of Jacob, whose hope is in the LORD his God, the Maker of heaven and earth, the sea, and everything in them—the LORD, who remains faithful forever. He upholds the

cause of the oppressed and gives food to the hungry. The LORD sets prisoners free, the LORD gives sight to the blind, the LORD lifts up those who are bowed down, the LORD loves the righteous.

—Psalm 146:5–8

June 20

I have given you many blessings. I pour out those blessings on all who love Me. No need to compare yourself with others because there is more than enough for you. I know it is your desire to give Me your first fruits, knowing it blesses Me. I AM your safety and your peace as you seek Me and put your trust in Me. Let your eyes and ears be open to see and hear that I AM doing a new thing. Look for the treasures; look for the insignificant events because I AM in those insignificant places. Get out of your box and let Me pour My blessings on you so you may be full and overflowing. Don't limit what I have for you—it's all yours!

And if you look for it as for silver and search for it as for hidden treasure, then you will understand the fear of the LORD and find the knowledge of God.

—Proverbs 2:4–5

June 21

Overcome your own tendencies in the flesh. Some are set up as patterns in your life as a way to communicate. Some fleshly desires are just a matter of choice. Choose rightly. Remember, I will give you the grace and all the power you need to overcome. Judge no one and do not be the lawyer in those relationships. It is I who judge a man's heart. Having a faultfinding and critical spirit can bring death to you and to all those who are in relationship with you. I desire that you would be My mouthpiece in a world that is hurting. Let Me heal the hurts in you so that those hurts don't hurt others. Your flesh must be crucified.

> My flesh and my heart may fail, but God is the strength of my heart and my portion forever.
> —Psalm 73:26

June 22

I have all your affairs and all your concerns in My hand. Rest, knowing I can do what seems to be impossible in your eyes. If you abide in Me and My words abide in you, you will ask what you desire and it shall be done for you. Remember, all is well despite what the circumstances look like. I AM an all-powerful, all-knowing, sovereign God and you can count on Me for everything. Trust and know this. Your faith will grow through these challenges.

Immediately the boy's father exclaimed, "I do believe; help me overcome my unbelief!"

—Mark 9:24

June 23

I AM blessing you, just receive it—don't question or doubt it. Don't worry if you fit in—don't even strive to fit in—just be yourself and give away My love. Be kind, be sure, be strong, and be a beacon of light to others. Man will always try to make you fit in a mold—resist it. Let Me flow freely and without reservation or restriction. Like a river flows, let My jewels flow where they will. Don't be concerned where the river goes, just follow it to Me. Like rain that falls, let My rain fill those dry places. Remember, the river flows in the valley, not on a mountaintop. Let My life flow where it will. Soak it up and walk in the ways I show you. Oh, how I love you!

There is a river whose streams make glad the city of God, the holy place where the Most High dwells.

—Psalm 46:4

June 24

My promises are true for you today. As you search My Word, you will see them written through and through. Look for them, claim them to be yours, and decree the promises over your life, your family, your marriage, your business, and anything else My hand is on. The road you travel can be one that narrows at times or widens at times, and you may even experience detours. Don't let any of the day-to-day travels stop you from receiving My promises. They are not based on circumstances. They are not based on feelings. My promises are based on My desire for you and My sacrifice on the cross that you may live and not die. Claim them afresh today! Claim them with hope! Claim them as a gold miner would claim his treasure.

> Yet he did not waver through unbelief regarding the promise of God, but was strengthened in his faith and gave glory to God, being fully persuaded that God had power to do what he had promised.
> —Romans 4:20–21

June 25

My blood has set you free. Do you believe this with all your heart? I want you to know there isn't anything My blood doesn't cover. Your freedom and our specific relationship were on My mind when I went to the cross. The world may bring back memories of your sins—even people you love might do the same. Know this: I do not remember your sins. It's not in My heart to do so. My blood has set you free, so you must know the past has no control over you. Move forward, receive My gift to you, and walk in complete freedom.

In him we have redemption through his blood, the forgiveness of sins, in accordance with the riches of God's grace that he lavished on us with all wisdom and understanding.

—Ephesians 1:7–9

June 26

Why do you strive so hard? Running here and there, trying to do this and that—hectic, chaotic, and tired. That is not My plan for you. Yes, there are many things that need to be done, but the most important is that you spend time with Me for your strategic plan of the day. Not all things you do are necessary. Not all things are wise or accomplish much—it's just busyness. I have promised you daily bread; I have promised you peace and rest. Come into My presence to hear My voice. Come into My presence to rest and know I AM God. Come to Me today to know what plans I have for you.

Many are the plans in a man's heart, but it is the LORD's purpose that prevails.

—Proverbs 19:21

June 27

Walk in humility. Honor and acknowledge those in your world who bless you today. Keep your eyes and heart open for opportunities to bless and love others. Just as I walked this earth healing and loving others, you too must reflect My life. I AM the only one who can bring hope, joy, peace, and security. I AM a shelter and refuge for you and those with whom you come in contact. Give, give, give everything you have received. Do not keep it for yourself. Let My love flow in and through you.

Show the wonder of your great love, you who save by your right hand those who take refuge in you from their foes.

—Psalm 17:7

June 28

Situations, people, and places don't always appear as you imagine. You have certain expectations that keep you closed off to new opportunities. It's hard to trust Me and others when you are not open to change. Situations change—some good, some bad, but they do change. People are people. Some hurt, some love, some reject, and some nourish. People are not all the same. Places, especially new places, can be intimidating and frightening. All in all, I AM the sovereign God who has it all in control. Put your hand in Mine and let Me gently guide your steps. My light will chase away any darkness in your life. Let My light shine brightly into all situations, people, and places.

Your eye is the lamp of your body. When your eyes are good, your whole body also is full of light. But when they are bad, your body also is full of darkness. See to it, then, that the light within you is not darkness. Therefore, if your whole body is full of light, and no part of it dark, it will be completely lighted, as when the light of a lamp shines on you.

—Luke 11:34–36

June 29

Smile and let your face reflect joy. As you look around in your comings and goings today, notice the faces of those with whom you come in contact. What do you see? Note how a frown can change a face. Note how a smile can change a face. Look to see if people hold their heads up high or if they walk looking down. Are their eyes bright or are they clouded by sorrow? Do they withdraw from you or are they open for a word of encouragement? I AM all they need. Let Me use you as My eyes, arms, and heart. Don't withhold anything.

You discern my going out and my lying down; you are familiar with all my ways. Before a word is on my tongue you know it completely, O LORD.

—Psalm 139:3–4

June 30

Do not be anxious for anything. Let My peace fill your heart. Experience it and know it to the depths of your heart. My peace will strengthen, My peace will comfort, and My peace will fill you with faith. My peace will help you along your journey, My peace will be your security, and My peace will cover everything. My peace will bring completeness and soundness into your life, My peace will give you a sense of well-being, and My peace will speak truth. My peace is God-given and assured. Take it and hold on to it.

> May the God of hope fill you with all joy and peace as you trust in him, so that you may overflow with hope by the power of the Holy Spirit.
> —Romans 15:13

JULY

July 1

WHO ARE YOU influencing today? Who is watching you and the decisions you are making moment by moment? Child, I want to use you to make an impact wherever you go. Are you aware of your surroundings or are you moving so fast that you don't stop to connect with those around you? Remember, today is all you have, this very moment. This is the *day* the Lord has made, will you rejoice in it? Ask yourself, how am I spending my time and how is it impacting the vision and dreams in my heart? Consider these things and re-evaluate where you are in this time of your life. Get on track if you got sidetracked. There is much more ahead of you, but it will only happen one step at a time. Believe anew.

The LORD your God is with you, he is mighty to save. He will take great delight in you, he will quiet you with his love, he will rejoice over you with singing.

—Zephaniah 3:17

July 2

Freedom is yours. Know that I died on the cross for your freedom. It was always My desire to have a relationship with you so you would not only know My love, but you would experience all the freedom that is yours. When you take a look around at all the blessings and breakthroughs in your life, know there is more light than darkness, more faith than doubt, more joy than pain, and more of Me and less of you. The cost of your freedom was My death. Oh, how I love you and how I need you to walk in all the promises I have given you.

The Spirit of the LORD is on me, because he has anointed me to preach good news to the poor. He has sent me to proclaim freedom for the prisoners and recovery of sight for the blind, to release the oppressed, to proclaim the year of the LORD's favor.

—Luke 4:18–19

July 3

When I see My children laughing, playing, dancing, and enjoying life, My heart leaps. God's children are free. When I see you walking in dominion and singing praises, it touches My heart. In the world's heaviness and burdens, one thing is sure: You can see the mark of My children. Why? Because you have what most people do not—a faith in a living God that brings life to you and others through our relationship. Never underestimate the power of My love. It is a love that not only transforms and reforms, but it will never run out. It is everlasting.

> So if you faithfully obey the commands I am giving you today—to love the LORD your God and to serve him with all your heart and with all your soul—then I will send rain on your land in its season, both autumn and spring rains, so that you may gather in your grain, new wine and oil. I will provide grass in the fields for your cattle, and you will eat and be satisfied.
>
> —Deuteronomy 11:13–15

July 4

In My presence is fullness of joy. My presence. Not just for the purpose of teaching, learning, serving, giving, or receiving. Just for the sake of being in My presence. Quiet, still, not distracted by daily requirements. Having your heart and your mind set on Me. Oh, what a delight that is for Me! Many pressures and chores pull on your daily life—I know and I understand. But it is in My presence where you will receive strength, hope, vision, direction, and peace. Take the time to be with Me. I AM waiting to pour out My love to you.

> You have made known to me the path of life; you will fill me with joy in your presence, with eternal pleasures at your right hand.
>
> —Psalm 16:11

July 5

Take a second look. What you have pondered or even known to be true might be different when you take that second look. I AM the same yesterday, today, and forever. I don't change. But you do. As you walk with Me day in and day out, your life and circumstances will look different. Your heart will be healed as I bring healing and wholeness to your soul. Your eyes will be healed. Your mind will be healed. Your body will be healed. Everything can change. Your sight can change in the way you see Me. Your ears can change in the way you hear Me. Consider taking that second look. You may be happily surprised.

> Look to the LORD and his strength; seek his face always. Remember the wonders he has done, his miracles, and the judgments he pronounced.
>
> —1 Chronicles 16:11–12

July 6

Trust Me in everything. Do not worry or fret about anything. I AM in control and you can rest knowing that truth. At times you question My ways and My timing. I understand that your soul gets troubled and concerned. Know that My love will comfort and protect you from worldly influences. Keep your eyes on Me. Keep your eyes on the goal. Do not be swayed by circumstances—they are only temporary and will change. Trust Me.

> To you, O LORD, I lift up my soul; in you I trust, O my God. Do not let me be put to shame, nor let my enemies triumph over me.
>
> —Psalm 25:1–2

July 7

My grace and mercy are sufficient for you. Quit striving. Choose to rest—it is needed. Come to Me. Quiet your soul. I will always be near. I love you. Can you hear Me? Let Me soften your heart. Let My presence touch you because My presence is beyond anything you could desire. Consider the sound of the river's trickle, the tender and gentle stream flowing. Let Me fill you in places where you are dry. Let Me be close to you. I want you to feel My embrace. I want you to know My touch.

This then is how we know that we belong to the truth, and how we set our hearts at rest in his presence whenever our hearts condemn us. For God is greater than our hearts, and he knows everything.

—1 John 3:19–20

July 8

Complications will steal your joy, so change your approach to life. Be determined to enjoy your life to the fullest. Keep it simple. Walk in faith and acknowledge Me in all your ways. My desire is that you live, laugh, and love those around you. Dance to the music, sing to the song, laugh in the moment, be free. I died so you could be free—not bound to this world but bound to all the promises I have for you. Do not live as the world lives. Live as My child with Me as your Father. Let Me pour out My love on you.

There is a time for everything, and a season for every activity under heaven ... a time to weep and a time to laugh, a time to mourn and a time to dance.

—Ecclesiastes 3:1, 4

July 9

Seek more of Me. Desire Me above all. The more you focus on Me, the less you will focus on the enemy's power in your life. Keep your eyes focused on the pure things in life. Just as the birds sing the minute the sun rises and there is light, know that your spirit will rise the moment you acknowledge the Light of the World. Wherever you lack wisdom, ask. Whenever you need revelation, ask. In circumstances where you need discernment, ask. I have all the power you need in all your ways. Seek and you will find.

> For the kingdom of God is not a matter of talk but of power.
>
> —1 Corinthians 4:20

July 10

Faith is not lived on the mountaintops of life. Faith is lived day in and day out, in the good and bad circumstances. Faith is believing in Me. Faith is knowing I AM, even when you do not know where you are going—like Abraham, who believed in Me and separated himself from all that was comfortable to live a life of faith. Many want to know and experience Me by sight, feelings, reasoning, assurance, and security. I want you to see Me through the eyes of faith. Separate yourself from the world and put your faith in Me. I AM leading and guiding you into all promise.

By faith Abraham, when called to go to a place he would later receive as his inheritance, obeyed and went, even though he did not know where he was going. By faith he made his home in the promised land like a stranger in a foreign country; he lived in tents, as did Isaac and Jacob, who were heirs with him of the same promise.

—Hebrews 11:8–9

July 11

I AM a deep well that never ends. Come and drink. What do you need today? Peace, rest, faith, courage, hope, life, financial provision? Come until you are filled. Come until you know I have touched your body, soul, and spirit. My sources are all you need. Drink deeply from the well.

But whoever drinks the water I give him will never thirst. Indeed, the water I give him will become in him a spring of water welling up to eternal life.

—John 4:14

July 12

Open your eyes to see My truths. Your mind, will, and emotions can distract you and lie to you. Do not depend on your worldly perspectives to direct your life. My Word and My truth are the only way. If you don't see, ask Me to show you. If you can't hear, be still so you can hear. I AM right here for you. I so desire to have our relationship grow deeper and deeper.

My eyes are ever on the LORD, for only he will release my feet from the snare.

—Psalm 25:15

July 13

You are empowered to succeed in all areas. You are strong, courageous, and bold. Remember, your past was defeated on the cross. Know that I remember no failures. Do not focus on those mistakes, regrets, or disappointments. The enemy of your soul wants to lie to you about your identity. You must know that you know that you are My child. Yes, you are in a war, but know this: I overcame it all!

Remember not the sins of my youth and my rebellious ways; according to your love remember me, for you are good, O LORD.

—Psalm 25:7

July 14

There are so many things I want to show you. There are so many wonders in My creation. As a child, you used to dream and imagine a life of joy. You wanted someone to hold you, talk to you, accept you, and love you. You had so many questions. Even if you had no one to show you those things growing up, I want you to know I AM here now to show you those things. Trust Me, My child—let's go on this journey together.

It is my pleasure to tell you about the miraculous signs and wonders that the Most High God has performed for me. How great are his signs, how mighty his wonders! His kingdom is an eternal kingdom; his dominion endures from generation to generation.

—Daniel 4:2–3

July 15

Storms may come, floods may come, and winds may come, but My Spirit will never overcome you. My Son is the bright light and He is in your life to shed truth. I created the world, the stars, the moon, and the entire universe. I know your comings and goings. I know the beginning from the end. I AM aware of the seasons in your life, so don't despise these happenings. Seasons come and seasons go. Trust Me with the season you are in today.

But I will sing of your strength, in the morning I will sing of your love; for you are my fortress, my refuge in times of trouble.

—Psalm 59:16

July 16

I want you to be more committed and count the cost. Many say one thing and do something different. Be someone who can be trusted and relied upon. That is My heart for you. Many have been hurt and wounded because of broken promises. My love and a life of integrity, character, and Christlikeness are what will bring transformation to those around you. Search My Word; learn of My character and My ways. A broken world needs to know My love. You are the vessel I want to flow through.

> May integrity and uprightness protect me, because my hope is in you.
>
> —Psalm 25:21

July 17

Do not worry about doing things perfectly. My love for you is not dependent on what you do or don't do. My love is based on who you are. You are My special child. Come and sit at My feet. Rest and let the world go by for a while. Your value is not based on what others think of you. It is based on who you are in Me. The world would want you to blend in and become like them. But know that I have called you out and separated you out for great things. So let go of all the ways you think you need to be perfect.

> As for God, his way is perfect; the word of the LORD is flawless. He is a shield for all who take refuge in him. For who is God besides the LORD? And who is the Rock except our God? It is God who arms me with strength and makes my way perfect.
>
> —Psalm 18:30–32

July 18

I AM a God of possibilities. I AM a God of faithfulness. I AM a God of comfort. I AM a God of protection. I AM a God that is trustworthy and true. I AM so much more to you than you could ever imagine. I will cover you with My feathers and I will protect you from the enemy. You can count on Me. I AM your refuge and safe place. Dwell in Me as I dwell in you. Come to Me whenever you need. I wait for My children to call My name.

> He will cover you with his feathers, and under his wings you will find refuge; his faithfulness will be your shield and rampart.
> —Psalm 91:4

July 19

Be an inspiration to someone today. As I have inspired you, you must inspire others. It won't take much effort. Just let My life and light shine through you. Open your eyes, open your ears, and you will know exactly who needs the word of life for today. As you have sought Me in your times of meditation and as you have heard My voice, give away what you have received. Darkness is all around the world. People are hopeless and faithless. People are afraid of the future. You have exactly what they need. Don't hide it or keep it for yourself. Let Me use you today.

Be joyful in hope, patient in affliction, faithful in prayer. Share with God's people who are in need. Practice hospitality.

—Romans 12:12–13

July 20

Strife and offense are a few of the tactics the enemy uses, and they always accomplish a separation between you and others. Many people are fearful, so staying in that offense somehow makes them feel safe from being hurt. They want intimacy but decide to stay separated and isolated so they don't risk rejection. Strife and offense are methods used to separate husband from wife, parents from children, and friends from friends. Some relationships even end permanently on a small offense, mainly due to misunderstandings. Stay open. Focus on the good and not the bad. Always be genuine and honest. Unity is the result. Remember, I have forgiven you, so you must forgive others.

He who covers over an offense promotes love, but whoever repeats the matter separates close friends.

—Proverbs 17:9

July 21

It's not life, circumstances, or relationships you have to conquer; it's only the self in you. You must learn to crucify self. Learn to walk in My ways. Know that I have given you all authority and power you need. It's Me you want. Claim all. It's available whenever you want it. A soldier would never go into war without power and authority from his superior. Walk forth in power. Crucify your old self and your old ways.

> For we know that our old self was crucified with him so that the body of sin might be done away with, that we should no longer be slaves to sin—because anyone who has died has been freed from sin.
>
> —Romans 6:6–7

July 22

Restoration is yours. Rest in Me. Expect great things. Keep things simple. Walk through your trials and tribulations with joy. Overcome the enemy and his lies. Let My resurrection life in you be shown to the world. Abide in Me and My Word. Trust that all is well. Initiate relationship with Me and others. Walk in obedience without wavering. Most of all, never ever give up! Tear down old structures and let Me bring restoration to you.

Restore to me the joy of your salvation and grant me
a willing spirit, to sustain me.

—Psalm 51:12

July 23

My grace is sufficient for you. Grace enables you
to do what you need to do and live like Me. My grace
is unmerited supernatural favor. Speak grace into
your situations, finances, marriage, and friendships.
Grace and peace go hand in hand. You have different
gifts provided to you through grace. Use them. I have
poured out My grace upon you abundantly. You will
never run out.

And God is able to make all grace abound to you,
so that in all things at all times, having all that you
need, you will abound in every good work.

—2 Corinthians 9:8

July 24

Put your hope in Me. Put down all your carnal
understandings and look to Me. Put all your dreams
and wishes in My hands. Live and breathe by My ways
and thoughts. Even before you were born, even before
you took your first breath, and even before you began to
see, hear, and smell, I knew you. I knitted you together
in your mother's womb. I created you for greatness. I
created you intricately and unique. Follow My words to

you. See how you touch others. Know I AM with you and I AM very proud of what I have created. I AM your Father and will always be your Father.

> The God who made the world and everything in it is the LORD of heaven and earth and does not live in temples built by hands. And he is not served by human hands, as if he needed anything, because he himself gives all men life and breath and everything else.
>
> —Acts 17:24–25

July 25

Your past will hold you down in chains. Your hurts, disappointments, and brokenness will pull you away from the plans I have for you. Come to Me as a child and let Me touch you in those places no other can reach. The world and its ways have no Savior or Comforter, but you do. Call on Me. Know that My grace heals. Know that My love will cover a multitude of sins. Come under that banner of love. Come to the well and drink. Let My healing balm bring you rest. I AM waiting for you.

> Then they cried to the LORD in their trouble, and he saved them from their distress. He brought them out of darkness and the deepest gloom and broke away their chains.
>
> —Psalm 107:13–14

July 26

What will it take to climb the mountain? What will you encounter along the way? At times it seems as though your current situation is a mountain to be climbed and the fear of falling can cause you to tremble. At times your situation can be overwhelming and too big for you to handle. I AM all you need to break through. I AM all you need to help you along the way. Yes, there may be stones that trip you up or boulders to stop you cold. But call on My name. I will give you the strategies you need. Nothing is impossible with Me.

> Every valley shall be raised up, every mountain and hill made low; the rough ground shall become level, the rugged places a plain. And the glory of the LORD will be revealed, and all mankind together will see it. For the mouth of the LORD has spoken.
> —Isaiah 40:4–5

July 27

Enjoy your life today. Don't wait until tomorrow or the next day. I gave you life to celebrate and enjoy. All those details in your life are important but not as important as spending time with Me. Rest and enjoy. Stop and be grateful. It's OK to rest and take care of yourself. Don't think that resting is a waste of time. It is life to you. Come and be refreshed in My presence. Come and seek My voice.

Be at rest once more, O my soul, for the LORD has been good to you.

—Psalm 116:7

July 28

Remember, I never sleep. I keep watch over you and every moment of your life. I created the universe and everything in it. I created you and everything you are made of. When times are tough or times are confusing, know I AM one who never sleeps. I AM the one who keeps you protected from harm. I AM the one who knows every detail of your life. I AM your shelter from the storm and so much more. Know Me and you will know My plans and purposes for your life.

He will not let your foot slip—he who watches over you will not slumber.

—Psalm 121:3

July 29

As you walk through your day today, be gentle to those around you. Desire to see them through My eyes and My heart rather than your own. Gentleness and kindness will cause your path to be smooth. Many are hurting, many are sad. Those around you need a touch of love, and you are the one I have chosen to pour out My love. I trust you with their hearts. I trust you with their care. Be gentle and kind. Remember those days when you needed a hug or a word of encouragement? Be My hands, My feet, and My heart to touch your world.

> Be completely humble and gentle; be patient, bearing with one another in love.
>
> —Ephesians 4:2

July 30

Notice the birds in the air. Notice how they flock together and fly together. That is My desire for you as well. When you try to fly alone and do things yourself, the burden can be too heavy. When you unite with others and work together, the burden is lifted and there is an ease that comes. Many of My children think if they have a need it is a sign of weakness. No, it is a sign of strength. I desire that My kingdom be strong and unified. It takes each one of you to unite with others. Don't fly alone.

> For none of us lives to himself alone and none of us dies to himself alone.
>
> —Romans 14:7

July 31

I AM the Master Potter and you are the clay. I AM in the process of creating a masterpiece. It doesn't happen overnight. It is a work that only begins when you first accept Me in your heart. My desire is that you would look just like Me. Sometimes it is a painful process and sometimes it is a resting process. Do not be dismayed. I love the fact that you are moldable and willing to be shaped into My nature. The smell and fragrance of a vessel that has been in the fire is a delight to Me and can change the world. Don't resist this time in your life. You will look back and know that My hands have been used to create a unique vessel for the Master's use.

> Does not the potter have the right to make out of the same lump of clay some pottery for noble purposes and some for common use?
>
> —Romans 9:21

AUGUST

August 1

I LOVE IT when you spend time with Me. I love it when above all else you make the time to be in relationship with Me. My heart leaps for joy when you call My name. I hear the requests, I hear the sighs, I understand the confusion. My children need a Father and I AM here for you whenever you call out My name. There are many gifts I want to give you—more than you could ever imagine. Not the gifts that the world can give, only gifts that come from My heart to yours. Stop and meditate on My Word to you today and let My love encircle you like a baby's blanket.

Give thanks to the LORD, call on his name; make known among the nations what he has done. Sing to him, sing praise to him; tell of all his wonderful acts. Glory in his holy name; let the hearts of those who seek the LORD rejoice.

—1 Chronicles 16:8–10

August 2

Sit at My feet and learn from Me. Let Me pour into you all truth and wisdom, not only for your life but for those around you. At the times when a friend is deeply hurting or in despair, it will be the wisdom I give you that will bring comfort. Let Me speak to your heart so when that time comes and people ask you where you get your strength, you will be able to tell them. Deep calls unto deep and there are many deep thoughts I want to share with you. Many say, "What a waste of time," but My words to you will bring life and breath to those who are hurting.

The LORD God has given me his words of wisdom so that I may know what I should say to all these weary ones. Morning by morning he wakens me and opens my understanding to his will.

—Isaiah 50:4 TLB

August 3

Climb that mountain, jump that river, build that house, and tackle those things that keep you from My presence. I AM everywhere and in every moment. What may look foolish to others is of no concern to you. Life with Me is adventurous and full of faith. Let Me unlock the gifts and dreams in your heart. Accomplish the things you have said were too hard. Overcome the obstacles. Don't only run the race but finish it. You can do all things you set your heart and mind to. Think of the many times I had to overcome. You have the same overcoming power living in you. Live life to its fullest. Do not delay.

> Build up, build up, prepare the road! Remove the obstacles out of the way of my people.
>
> —Isaiah 57:14

August 4

You are My prized possession. I knitted you in your mother's womb. I took all the time, effort, and skill to create you just the way I wanted you. I thought of every detail and designed you perfect in My eyes. There was not one thing I left out. You were created in My image. You are My handiwork and My greatest joy. When you doubt your value, all you have to know is that there is not one flaw in you that would change the way I see you. Just as a potter gracefully and with great skill creates his beautiful creation, I too spent all the time needed to create the way you are. Accept yourself. Love all that I love. Never again doubt your worth.

> Then the word of the LORD came to me: "O house of Israel, can I not do with you as this potter does?" declares the LORD. "Like clay in the hand of the potter, so are you in my hand, O house of Israel."
> —Jeremiah 18:5–6

August 5

Look to this day with great joy and expectation. I have a surprise for you, but you must be expectant and looking for it. It won't be in the way that you think. It won't look the way you think it should. It won't sound like the way you normally listen. Open your heart, ears, and eyes in a fresh new way. Many go throughout their day with very little joy. It becomes ho-hum and just normal to them, day after day. But know this: today will be a defining day for you. Expect it.

> You also must be ready, because the Son of Man will come at an hour when you do not expect him.
> —Luke 12:40

August 6

Let your heart be healthy, in the physical as well as the spiritual. Don't carry the hurts and offenses of the past. Don't walk around with burdens and unforgiveness in your soul. Forgive and forget. Let Me heal your hurts and bind up your wounds. I want you to be a witness to a lost and broken world, but you must first let Me touch your life. Let My healing balm bring healing and wholeness to your soul. Don't hide from Me, but come running to Me with all that concerns you. The longer you wait, the deeper the pain. Come swiftly to Me.

They are free from the burdens common to man; they are not plagued by human ills.

—Psalm 73:5

August 7

In one moment, your life can change. In one moment, your dream can be broken. In one moment, your reality as you know it can become very different. Many waste their days thinking that another day will be different. Too many times your heart is looking backward or forward and you entirely miss the moments I have planned for you. My promise to you is that I will provide manna one day at a time. Come and live today to its fullest, because what I have for you is enough. Live this moment with purpose. Live this day with gratitude and thankfulness. It's all you have right now—this very moment.

So then, just as you received Christ Jesus as LORD, continue to live in him, rooted and built up in him, strengthened in the faith as you were taught, and overflowing with thankfulness.

—Colossians 2:6–7

August 8

Even as you see the clouds and the rain in the natural, know there is a higher purpose for everything I do. Look at the fruit of what rain and clouds can mean in the natural. Even as you apply the clouds and the rain in your life today, know they also have a purpose for you. Even in times of oppression and heaviness, My Spirit can bring you hope. Even when the storms come and go, I can restore everything that was damaged. I AM known to many as the Repairer of the Breach and the Restorer. I will bring you comfort as you put your trust in Me. Know that everything has its purpose and plan. Look up and see the Son. Look up and know that even in the midst of the clouds, there is always a rainbow. You just need to put your trust in Me.

You have been a refuge for the poor, a refuge for the needy in his distress, a shelter from the storm and a shade from the heat.

—Isaiah 25:4

August 9

I AM your hiding place. I AM your protector in times of trouble. I surround you with songs of victory, and the battles are won. When you are weary and tired, seek Me. When you are fearful or anxious about circumstances, seek Me. All soldiers need a time of rest. Come to Me. Hide in the shadows of My wings and rest. You are a general in My army and you need that time to get your marching orders. Don't ever go into battle ill equipped. I AM by your side, but I also want you to know the specific strategies. Come, put on your armor and let's move out.

You are my hiding place; you will protect me from trouble and surround me with songs of deliverance.
—Psalm 32:7

August 10

Tap into My wisdom. Tap into My voice. Exercise your senses—all of them. I speak in ways you haven't even tapped into. Stay in awe of Me and who I AM. Take down any and all limitations you have put on Me. Expand your tent pegs. Value what I value. Oh, how I want to pour My wisdom into you—not as the world sees, but how I see. Widen and deepen the way you see Me. I AM unpredictable and significant in the days to come. Make time for Me and you will begin to understand My ways.

The fear of the LORD is the beginning of wisdom, and knowledge of the Holy One is understanding. For through me your days will be many, and years will be added to your life.

—Proverbs 9:10–11

August 11

Draw near to Me as I draw near to you. Draw closer and closer each day. Remember, it is only through My death on the cross that you have freedom. I paid the ultimate cost for you and I desire to have an intimate relationship with you. Intimacy with Me is not about perfection or works; it's about spending time with Me. Make it a priority today. Oh, if you only would understand and know My heart for you!

Let us draw near to God with a sincere heart in full assurance of faith, having our hearts sprinkled to cleanse us from a guilty conscience and having our bodies washed with pure water.

—Hebrews 10:22

August 12

Rise up and stand firm. Rise up in the midst of trials and tribulations. Stand firm on My Word and My promises to you. When you want to lie down, give up, and get discouraged, My desire for you is to rise up and stand firm. Stand firm on the Rock. Nothing will shatter or destroy you. I AM the same yesterday, today, and tomorrow. I never change. It's My saving power that will rescue you. Just believe, and put your hope not only in what I can do for you but, more importantly, who I AM for you. Come to know Me in a deeper way.

> Some trust in chariots and some in horses, but we trust in the name of the LORD our God. They are brought to their knees and fall, but we rise up and stand firm.
>
> —Psalm 20:7–8

August 13

Do not let divisions come between you and others. Divisions cause separation and pain. My desire is that you would walk in unity; not just with other believers but with others who don't know Me. The world is looking to you to give them answers to their situations and pain today. You must discern the times and know My voice. When you let minor setbacks cause you to focus on yourself and not on others, My heart cries. The world wants to know what you have. They are hungry. In these perilous times, they are fearful and insecure. Keep your hearts in unity with one another and reach out to a hurting and dying world. Be My hands and feet.

> May the God who gives endurance and encourage-
> ment give you a spirit of unity among yourselves as

you follow Christ Jesus, so that with one heart and mouth you may glorify the God and Father of our LORD Jesus Christ.

—Romans 15:5–6

August 14

Peace to you—abundant peace. Peace like the still waters. Peace like a quiet river. Peace that overrides your current situation. That is My desire for you. Make peace with others. Make peace with yourself. Nothing or no one can give you the peace I can give you. I AM peace, and you can have it just for the asking. Seek strength and peace today.

The LORD gives strength to his people; the LORD blesses his people with peace.

—Psalm 29:11

August 15

Prosperity is here and now. There is a wonderful life of prosperity waiting for you. Not prosperity as the world knows it, but prosperity from My throne of grace. Prosperity in the spirit, prosperity in relationships, prosperity in health, prosperity in business, prosperity in finances—prosperity in all things. What does it mean to be prosperous? It means to flourish and thrive in all I have created for you to have. It is your inheritance. Stop and listen today for all the ways you can prosper.

> Submit to God and be at peace with him; in this way prosperity will come to you. Accept instruction from his mouth and lay up his words in your heart.
> —Job 22:21–22

August 16

Where there is darkness, I will bring in light. You have all it takes to change your world. You are full of love and you know whom you are, so reach out today. Be that light in the midst of whatever darkness you see. Darkness will never overpower light. I AM the Light of the World, and that light is in you. It is a light that makes everything visible. Don't hide it under a bushel or let it go out. It only takes a flicker to impact those around you. Arise, shine, and be that light to the world—one by one.

> I will lead the blind by ways they have not known; along unfamiliar paths I will guide them; I will turn the darkness into light before them and make the rough places smooth.
> —Isaiah 42:16

August 17

The storms, trials, and struggles in your past shall pass away and I will do a new thing in you. I AM doing a new thing at this very moment. Remember My words: "It is finished." Settle it once and for all. Let My glory and presence speak to all the details in your heart so I can bring transformation. No longer will you have to walk in shackles. I have set you free. Just as a prisoner is bound to his personal circumstances, know you are free from all that binds you. I finished it all on the cross. Do not doubt in your heart, do not live in the past, and do not walk as if it holds you back. I have done great things for you. Walk in total freedom.

> Set me free from my prison, that I may praise your name. Then the righteous will gather about me because of your goodness to me.
>
> —Psalm 142:7

August 18

As you step out today, know My presence and power are with you. You have done all you can. Now is the time to put total trust in Me and see the Lord's glory. I love that you care so deeply and desire to help others. I love that you seek Me and My heart in all situations. I love that you hear My voice and obey. Now is the time for you to stand and wait.

Now then, stand still and see this great thing the LORD is about to do before your eyes!

—1 Samuel 12:16

August 19

There are many gates opening for you. There are many opportunities to choose from. I have made a way where there doesn't seem to be a way. The gates are open, the doors have swung wide open, and it is your time of victory. There have been so many desires in your heart for more. The more has arrived! It is My great pleasure to pour out My blessings on you. In the past, those gates might have been closed. But today, they are wide open for you to walk in and through. Walk boldly and with confidence. This is your day!

Pass through, pass through the gates! Prepare the way for the people. Build up, build up the highway! Remove the stones. Raise a banner for the nations.

—Isaiah 62:10

August 20

Do not doubt My hand in your life. Believe that it is My great pleasure to bless you. Doubt causes confusion, unbelief, and stress in your life that you don't need. Others in your life need you to be strong, clear minded, courageous, and focused on My plans. Doubt only causes your life's foundation to rattle and shake, which only causes others to be fearful. I have placed great responsibility in your hands and I will be faithful to make sure those plans are accomplished. Believe Me in all your ways.

> But when he asks, he must believe and not doubt, because he who doubts is like a wave of the sea, blown and tossed by the wind.
>
> —James 1:6

August 21

Stay in tune with your heart. Out of the issues of the heart, the mouth speaks. Life can be hard. People say things they don't mean, and what they say can affect your life for the better or for the worse. You have the ability to guard your heart. The heart you have is the one I have given you, so protect it from the outside world. Keep it open; just be wise in what you allow in. Many are wounded because of words spoken. Be someone who only blesses and does not curse others. It is a matter of life or death. Let your heart sing and anything that comes from that place will bring love and life.

> Above all else, guard your heart, for it is the wellspring of life. Put away perversity from your mouth; keep corrupt talk far from your lips.
>
> —Proverbs 4:23–24

August 22

Your destiny is in My hands. My plans and purposes are sure and strong. Everything you have walked through up to this point has been preparation time. There were many times you thought I had abandoned you or didn't even care about you. I understand. But just as a Father parents a child, I too have had to parent you in ways that were hard at times. Love hurts but love is all powerful. My love for you is deep, wide, and high—more than you can ever imagine. I chasten only those I love. You are My child and I will never stop loving you!

No discipline seems pleasant at the time, but painful. Later on, however, it produces a harvest of righteousness and peace for those who have been trained by it.

—Hebrews 12:11

August 23

With Me all things are possible. With Me all things work for good. I restore all things. I AM committed to all things. All things in heaven and on earth are yours. All things—I mean "all things." Take courage. I AM the creator of all things. I AM all you ever will need. I AM capable of transforming everything. I AM that I AM and nothing is impossible for Me. Life without Me is impossible to enjoy. Life with Me is full of joy, hope, love, peace, rest, and a future that will always be bright. Never doubt or step away from Me. You may not understand everything; that's OK. Just continue to put your trust in Me. I AM faithful and true.

> For by him all things were created: things in heaven and on earth, visible and invisible, whether thrones or powers or rulers or authorities; all things were created by him and for him. He is before all things, and in him all things hold together.
> —Colossians 1:16–17

August 24

Bring your offerings to Me. Bring all you are and all you do to Me. Lay it all down at My feet. Bring all that concerns you to Me. Come and worship Me in a new, fresh, living way. Do not hold on to old ideas, old ways of doing things, old hurts, or old mindsets. Come and bring all your burdens to Me. Man was not created to be burdened with the issues of life. Offer everything to Me. There are issues in your family I want you to give Me. There are financial struggles in your life I want you to surrender to Me. There are places in your heart that need My healing touch, but you must first come and offer your heart to Me. Offerings and thankfulness go hand in hand. Once surrendered to Me, you can be assured of freedom and liberty.

Be imitators of God, therefore, as dearly loved children and live a life of love, just as Christ loved us and gave himself up for us as a fragrant offering and sacrifice to God.

—Ephesians 5:1–2

August 25

I AM your sustainer in the desert. I AM living water in the wilderness. I will make rivers in the dry wasteland so you will be refreshed. When your life seems dry and lifeless, know that even that season can bring much fruit. My rivers will flow on the barren heights and I will open a spring in the midst of you. Don't run from what I AM trying to do. As you endure for a night, My joy will come in the morning. I have a track for you to walk, and wherever it goes, you will be OK. Don't try to analyze or reason this specific time, but know this: I will carry you through to the best of times. I will be your oasis in the desert.

He turned the desert into pools of water and the parched ground into flowing springs; there he brought the hungry to live, and they founded a city where they could settle.

—Psalm 107:35–36

August 26

Keep your eyes on Me and I will rescue you from your enemies' traps. I AM strong and mighty in battle. The battle is Mine. Remain confident that I can do it. Whenever you are in trouble, call on Me. I AM your refuge and strength. The enemy wants to steal, kill, and destroy your seed. Keep sowing. The enemy wants to steal, kill, and destroy your family. Give your family to Me. The enemy wants to steal, kill, and destroy your finances. Keep giving. The enemy wants to steal, kill, and destroy your joy. Be joyous anyway. No weapon formed against you will prosper. Sing praises to My name and for the mighty work I AM doing.

> This is what the LORD says: "Heaven is my throne, and the earth is my footstool. Where is the house you will build for me? Where will my resting place be? Has not my hand made all these things, and so they came into being?" declares the LORD.
>
> —Isaiah 66:1–2

August 27

My grace covers you and penetrates through all your problems and shortcomings. Whenever you make a mistake, My grace covers it. If you trip and fall, My grace will pick you up. If you get wounded or hurt by others, My grace will heal you. If you get confused and insecure about who you are, My grace will fill you. My grace is unmerited favor. Just receive it and wear it like a glove. Welcome My grace, live in My grace, swim in My grace, and enter into My grace like a refreshing waterfall. Let it splash all over you. My grace is a manifestation of love and My love endures forever.

> The grace of our LORD was poured out on me abundantly, along with the faith and love that are in Christ Jesus.
>
> —1 Timothy 1:14

August 28

Be strong and courageous today. Let your light shine in a world that is desperate and fearful. Many are seeking Me but are on a path that leads to destruction. Many want to know My love, but their hearts are shut off to Me. Many are weary and tired and ready to give up. The death and depression in My people is great in these perilous times. Let your smile and heart touch those in your presence. You don't know who is watching you and your actions. Because you are a vessel of righteousness, My hands and feet, ask for wisdom and discernment in how to touch a troubled world. I will guide and direct your path. Love and give away all I have given you.

I guide you in the way of wisdom and lead you along straight paths. When you walk, your steps will not be hampered; when you run, you will not stumble. Hold on to instruction, do not let it go; guard it well, for it is your life.

—Proverbs 4:11–13

August 29

Double for your trouble. I will repay two blessings for each of your troubles. I AM planting seeds of peace and prosperity among you. You are a generation of great blessings. Your land will produce abundant crops. Your garden will bloom and flourish. Wherever you go and whatever you do will be blessed. I will bless wherever you place your hands. Your children and their children will be blessed. Your vats will run over. Abundant living will be yours. Many don't realize how much I want to bless them. All I want you and all my other children to do is simply obey My voice and follow My commandments. It's that simple.

The blessing of the LORD brings wealth, and he adds no trouble to it.

—Proverbs 10:22

August 30

Worship Me. Worship Me in the morning, worship Me in the evening, worship Me at all times. Worship Me in spirit and in truth. Worship and praise My name in all circumstances. Let it be a joyful praise. Let it be a praise of freedom and liberty. Let it flow freely from your heart. Worship Me with all of your body, soul, and spirit. Be still and worship. Worship the One who lives forever and ever.

> Yet a time is coming and has now come when the true worshipers will worship the Father in spirit and truth, for they are the kind of worshipers the Father seeks. God is spirit, and his worshipers must worship in spirit and in truth.
>
> —John 4:23–24

August 31

Don't judge others by their appearance or height. Many have been wounded by judgment. Because of that hurt, many have judged others. The law of judgment brings disunity, jealousy, pride—all the works of the flesh. Judge not, lest you be judged. It is a very valuable lesson to learn in your walk with Me. When My sons and daughters hurt each other, My heart breaks. Judgment of others is the enemy's work to bring separation between people and separation between others and Me. It is an evil work. Keep your heart pure and without judgment. I AM the only Lawgiver and Judge.

Do not judge, or you too will be judged. For in the same way you judge others, you will be judged, and with the measure you use, it will be measured to you.

—Matthew 7:1–2

SEPTEMBER

September 1

DESPERATION. DEFERRED HOPES and dreams. Broken promises. Health concerns. Financial debt. Wayward children. Many things to distract you from Me. I understand. This life is hard and sometimes it does feel hopeless. Tears shed, laughter comes once again. Darkness, and then the light shines brightly. Remember that no matter what this life throws at you, I AM your refuge from the storm. I AM the shelter from the winds. I AM the safe place and your comfort. I AM all you need even though at times it doesn't feel like it's enough. I know. That's when the truth of who I AM has to take precedence over what you feel. Let your spirit rise and let your soul rest. In days to come, you won't even remember the concerns of today. Trust in Me completely today.

But you will cross the Jordan and settle in the land the LORD your God is giving you as an inheritance, and he will give you rest from all your enemies around you so that you will live in safety.

—Deuteronomy 12:10

September 2

Empty your mind of all that limits you. Open your heart to Me and the possibilities in front of you. Your future is not based on your past mistakes. Your future is not dependent on others' limitations. Your future is based on My Word and My destiny for you. Don't look to the world or your circumstances to define what your future may be. I have higher ways and higher plans for you. Be careful that your thought life does not limit or stop you from walking into the fullness I have for you. Clear your mind and open your heart to My plans. They will be grand and glorious!

But the plans of the LORD stand firm forever, the purposes of his heart through all generations.

—Psalm 33:11

September 3

I have made a covenant with you because I AM a covenant-keeping God. This is a covenant of unconditional love, peace, and joy. A covenant cannot be broken. It is a promise and commitment to love you and do good to you. The world breaks covenants because they look at them more as a contract than a promise. There is nothing you can ever do that will break the covenant I have with you. It is your assurance of safety, protection, and a full life.

> I will make a covenant of peace with them; it will be an everlasting covenant. I will establish them and increase their numbers, and I will put my sanctuary among them forever. My dwelling place will be with them; I will be their God, and they will be my people.
>
> —Ezekiel 37:26–27

September 4

My Word stands forever. The words I have spoken to you today, yesterday, and years before stand. Revisit what I have spoken to you. Reexamine what the heart of the words has meant to you. Look at those words that have not come true as of today and ask Me why. Just as a father and mother desire to instruct and guide their children, I too want to instruct you in the ways of the Lord. I don't ever change My mind, and I don't ever speak things unless I know there is power for those things to happen. Temporary things change and wither away, but the Word of the Lord stands forever. Know that and trust My words to you.

> The grass withers and the flowers fall, but the word of our God stands forever.
>
> —Isaiah 40:8

September 5

I AM calling you to come up higher. I AM calling you to fly higher into the depths of My Spirit. I AM all you need. I have so many things to show you about who I AM and what My kingdom has to offer. Many try to understand spiritual things but can't because they can't see with spiritual eyes. I want to give you eyes to see Me and My kingdom differently. I desire to pour out My Spirit on you in a fresh, new way. Just like a lake without an inlet can go stale, you too can slow the flow of My Spirit. It always has to be moving. If you know what is blocking the flow, remove it quickly. If you desire to spend more time with Me, change your plans. Rivers flow from here to there with little trouble, so let My Spirit flow without complications.

> Swarms of living creatures will live wherever the river flows. There will be large numbers of fish, because this water flows there and makes the salt water fresh; so where the river flows everything will live.
>
> —Ezekiel 47:9

September 6

Don't let your emotions take precedence over the truth. Be careful about your thoughts. Watch out for the words you speak. Communicating out of a place of hurt and woundedness will only bring more hurt. There are places in your heart where you haven't forgiven completely. There are signs along the way that you have made judgments and criticized the ones you love. Oh, how the enemy of your soul would love for you to give up and run away! Come back to Me for guidance. Come to My secret place so I can bring healing to your heart. Remember, this isn't a setback; this is a time to move forward. Come to Me.

> Do not let your hearts be troubled. Trust in God; trust also in me. In my Father's house are many rooms; if it were not so, I would have told you. I am going there to prepare a place for you.
>
> —John 14:1–2

September 7

Remember when you were a child and the wind was blowing in your hair, a smile was on your face, and joy was coming from your heart? Remember when there was only innocence and hope for the future? There was excitement about the next adventure, excitement about the next birthday, and excitement about seeing your friends. Where did the laughter and joy go? What have your disappointments and discouragements stolen from you? Remember, I will always be your Friend, your Teacher, your Laughter, your Joy, your Hope, your Comforter, your greatest encourager, and so much more. Let the joy bubble up above all the hurt. Smile again from the inside out.

Be merciful to me, O Lord, for I am in distress; my eyes grow weak with sorrow, my soul and my body with grief. My life is consumed by anguish and my years by groaning; my strength fails because of my affliction, and my bones grow weak.

—Psalm 31:9–10

September 8

Be free to take off your masks. No shame, no fear, no doubt, no sense of unworthiness. Be who I have created you to be. See yourself through My eyes. When you were in your mother's womb, I thought of every detail. I knitted every part of you and your life uniquely and with great pleasure. Let rest and peace come to your soul. Don't look to others and compare. Don't measure yourself through the world's eyes. Only measure yourself from the eyes of the One who loves you and created you for His great pleasure. Everything about you is beautiful and My eyes are permanently fixed on you!

He will swallow up death forever. The Lord God will wipe away all tears and take away forever all insults and mockery against his land and people. The Lord has spoken—he will surely do it! In that day the people will proclaim, "This is our God in whom we trust, for whom we waited. Now at last he is here." What a day of rejoicing!

—Isaiah 25:8–9 TLB

September 9

I AM the Father to the fatherless, a defender of widows. I put you in family wherever you go. The kingdom family is there to love you, encourage you, build you up, disciple you, and help you along the way. My children will never be left alone, fatherless, or lonely. That is My plan. When others have rejected you, betrayed you, or made you feel insignificant, know that it is I who call you My child. I too was rejected and betrayed by those I loved. My Father was always by My side just the same way I AM by your side. Never forget the greater plans and purposes I have for you. We are family!

A father to the fatherless, a defender of widows, is God in his holy dwelling. God sets the lonely in families, he leads forth the prisoners with singing; but the rebellious live in a sun-scorched land.

—Psalm 68:5–6

September 10

No matter what you try, you feel there is no hope. Things don't change. Situations are out of your control. It's a place of deep concern and hopelessness. As hard as you try to pick yourself up, it seems to be a struggle. I understand. I cry when you cry. I feel sorrow when you are sorrowful. I have experienced the range of emotions through which you are walking. I know the sorrow; I know the joy. Don't give up. Don't fall into old thought patterns that would bring destruction to you and your family. Come away with Me. Take time to be with Me today. Stop and listen to My voice. I know it's hard, but it is extremely important.

> Take away the disgrace I dread, for your laws are good. How I long for your precepts! Preserve my life in your righteousness.
> —Psalm 119:39–40

September 11

Live your life based on the calling I have given you. Let the fruit of My Spirit live in and through you. I have called you and I have anointed you. Be patient, be kind, and be humble and forgiving. Lay down your life for others. Become the greatest servant of all. What others do and what others say should have no impact on you. My heart lives within you and My life is all you need. All you need is yours. You have no lack. There are no prison walls. You are free to be you. Release yourself from your past and walk into the future I have for you.

> As a prisoner for the LORD, then, I urge you to live a life worthy of the calling you have received. Be completely humble and gentle; be patient, bearing with one another in love. Make every effort to keep the unity of the Spirit through the bond of peace.
> —Ephesians 4:1–3

September 12

I need mothers and fathers to re-parent the children of this world. I need the wisdom and experience you have to pour out to a generation that is tired and lost—a generation that has no boundaries, a generation that doubts My love and power in their lives. I need you to step up to that rightful place and nurture those in your surroundings. Just as I have nurtured you, you must nurture others. The world of this age has lost the importance and significance of a father and mother. I AM their one and only Father and I AM the only one who can nurture and love them. You must be My heart, My arms, My mouth, and an ambassador of My love. Open your eyes and see who needs My touch today. Tenderly care for them and cultivate a relationship with them.

> Though my father and mother forsake me, the LORD will receive me.
>
> —Psalm 27:10

September 13

Be willing to do the little things. Maybe you know someone who needs a ride. Maybe someone needs help with paying the electric bill. Maybe there is someone who just needs a simple phone call or a card to brighten up his or her day. Small things can become big things to others. When was the last time you called and prayed for someone who was on your mind? When was the last time you bought a meal for someone—not out of obligation but from a place of a giving heart? There are those who need that word or hug or smile today. Take time to give what you have.

> Therefore, as God's chosen people, holy and dearly loved, clothe yourselves with compassion, kindness, humility, gentleness and patience.
> —Colossians 3:12

September 14

Not everything that looks good is good for you. Not everything that comes your way is My purpose or plan. There are many decisions, many ideas, and many ways to walk, but the best way is My way. Ask Me and hear My voice for the best. I walk before you and, at times, you will notice I will carry you. Decide today to walk upright with love in your heart. Keep your walk pure and blameless before Me. Your safety and protection are in My hands. Ask Me for the truth. Stay in touch with Me in every aspect of your life and put your trust in Me. I will never lead you astray, My child.

> He holds victory in store for the upright; he is a shield to those, whose walk is blameless, for he guards the course of the just and protects the way of his faithful ones.
> —Proverbs 2:7–8

September 15

Do not shrink back from responsibilities. Do not let circumstances overwhelm you and allow the spirit of fear to enter in. I have equipped you for great things and I have covered you with strength—not as the world sees strength but as I see strength. Continue to praise Me, continue to walk in My joy, and continue to stay in a place of thankfulness and walk in My love. I have empowered you to conquer all the barriers you face. You are a mighty warrior. Know that the battle is Mine and not yours. Surrender it all to Me and walk boldly with courage.

But we are not of those who shrink back and are destroyed, but of those who believe and are saved.
—Hebrews 10:39

September 16

Take a deep breath and stay calm. Calmness can happen in the midst of the storm. In the midst of a hurricane, it is a known fact that the middle of the storm is the calmest place. So when agitated or troubled, let Me give you the ability to stay calm. I will help you have the right perspective. Many wrong decisions can be made from a place of frustration, agitation, or fear. Sometimes those decisions can be life changing. When you allow panic to rule your life, nothing can bring you to a place of calm. Stop before you let yourself get troubled and take a deep breath. I AM your safe place and I can calm the seas. Let My peace rule in your life.

They were glad when it grew calm, and he guided them to their desired haven. Let them give thanks to the LORD for his unfailing love and his wonderful deeds for men.

—Psalm 107:30–31

September 17

You are My greatest miracle. You are unique, created to do only what you can do. Miracles happen day and night, but there is no greater miracle than your birth. When you keep your eyes on others, compare yourself with others, compete with others, or feel insecure about your capabilities, you discount what I have created in you. I created you exactly the way you are. Don't let shame or inferiority dictate your behavior or identity. What I create is special, unique, and a gift to the world. Consider yourself that gift. Give it freely.

Every good and perfect gift is from above, coming down from the Father of the heavenly lights, who does not change like shifting shadows. He chose to give us birth through the word of truth that we might be a kind of firstfruits of all he created.

—James 1:17–18

September 18

Hear My voice clearly today. Open your eyes wide and see clearly today. There are distractions and plans that the enemy is using to bring destruction. Do not be naive about the small and seemly insignificant ploys. He has an agenda to separate you from others and to separate you from Me. One of his tactics is selfishness. If he can keep you focused on him or on the disappointments, then he can lie to you. If you buy into his tactics, the door is open for other lies. The battle is on. Make sure to keep your battle guard on. Know that I conquered death on the cross so that you may have life. Choose life and truth. Put on the whole armor of God and keep it on.

> When you go into battle in your own land against an enemy who is oppressing you, sound a blast on the trumpets. Then you will be remembered by the LORD your God and rescued from your enemies.
> —Numbers 10:9

September 19

Endure suffering as a good soldier of Christ Jesus. What does that actually mean to you? Remember that civilians do not get tied up or caught up in the affairs or circumstances of their lives. Soldier? What does it take to be My soldier? First of all, it takes a willingness to submit to Me. It takes a determination to be the best you can be. It takes a sacrifice of time, talent, gifts, and the willingness to suffer. But most of all, it takes your heart. There are many good things a soldier carries out, but the greatest assignment is the servant-like attitude. Dangers loom around you daily—it takes a soldier My hands have trained to know exactly how to handle the situations. Get trained, stay trained, and then train others.

> Endure hardship with us like a good soldier of Christ Jesus. No one serving as a soldier gets involved in civilian affairs—he wants to please his commanding officer.
>
> —2 Timothy 2:3–4

September 20

The world says beauty is in the eye of the beholder. In My kingdom, the truth is that beauty begins from the inside out. Beauty comes from the ability to know and experience a love that is so deep, so rich, so long lasting, and so true. Beauty is an inside job. As I touch your heart, as I bring healing to your hurts, and as I reveal the truth that counteracts the lie, a fragrance begins to fill the air. It is the beauty of My righteousness. Outside beauty is shallow, but one who fears the Lord is to be praised. So today, let Me help you redefine what beauty means to you. It's so much more than what the world dictates.

Your beauty should not come from outward adorn-
ment, such as braided hair and the wearing of gold
jewelry and fine clothes. Instead, it should be that of
your inner self, the unfading beauty of a gentle and
quiet spirit, which is of great worth in God's sight.

—1 Peter 3:3–4

September 21

There are many directions from which you can
choose. Even as you travel from here to there, you will
notice different road signs that mean different things. One
may say, "Stop"; one may say, "Go." One may indicate
a bump is ahead, and yet another may indicate there are
deer in the area. There are many signs and help along
the way to maneuver the journey. Man has attempted to
help man with the best available. I, too, have many signs
to follow. My desire is that you choose life along the way
and not follow signs that would lead to destruction. My
voice is a sign. My Word is a sign. My servants can be
part of the sign. Follow Me and I will not lead you astray.
Believe in the direction I AM leading you.

Jesus did many other miraculous signs in the presence
of his disciples, which are not recorded in this book.
But these are written that you may believe that Jesus
is the Christ, the Son of God, and that by believing
you may have life in his name.

—John 20:30–31

September 22

Keep your eyes focused on Me. Do not worry about the days ahead. Do not be anxious about anything today. I want you to experience peace in all that you do. Peace as still as a lake where there is no breeze—it's not a place of staleness but a place of assurance and stillness in Me. Peace can heal your heart. Peace can calm your emotions. Peace can shed light on My truth. Many run here and there, tired and weary. Do not rush My hand or My ways. Rest assured that I AM on track, never early and never late. Right on track. Peace be still.

> "Though the mountains be shaken and the hills be removed, yet my unfailing love for you will not be shaken nor my covenant of peace be removed," says the LORD, who has compassion on you.
>
> —Isaiah 54:10

September 23

Kindness is needed today. Simple, loving acts toward others are needed today. A simple smile can make a difference. Many have turned their focus on themselves and their situations and have shut others out. I do not want you to become numb and familiar with the simplicity of your life. I AM always doing a new thing and I desire that you pay attention to the new thing. Oh, what a spectacular life you have. Even the simplest things can be the most profound. It's your heart attitude toward those things that can change your perspective. Give away your love and kindness. You will never be sorry.

> I led them with cords of human kindness, with ties of love; I lifted the yoke from their neck and bent down to feed them.
>
> —Hosea 11:4

September 24

I created you uniquely. Everything about you was created special. I have created every detail of your life. I AM the One to give you strength and I AM the One to give you wisdom. I AM all you need. Because of your uniqueness, I have called you to be unique in all your gifting. I have established you in a place that is uniquely your own. I have guided your path in a unique and fruitful plan. I have thought of it all. There is not one aspect of your life of which I AM not aware. Put your trust in your Creator. Your fingerprint is unique and identifiable.

> He chose to give us birth through the word of truth, that we might be a kind of firstfruits of all he created.
>
> —James 1:18

September 25

You are My child who is bold and courageous. When My Word says "fear not" that does not mean you won't experience fear. It means do what I have called you to do, even if you feel afraid. I understand fear. I too experienced fear, but I was always obedient to what My Father wanted Me to do. Fear does not have to stop you. Even in the midst of that fear, know you can always feel assured of My presence in your life. You will always overcome anything that tries to stop you through fear. If I have called you to do it, do it.

> He will have no fear of bad news; his heart is steadfast, trusting in the LORD. His heart is secure, he will have no fear; in the end he will look in triumph on his foes.
> —Psalm 112:7–8

September 26

Deception can be a trap. It is always a lie and it wants to cause pain. You may not always see or know the truth. You may not always see the entire picture. Some pieces could be missing and some may be hidden from sight. There can be blind spots in your life, so do not depend on your senses. My ways are higher and My ways will always lead to truth. It's a daily walk with Me to find truth. Stay connected to Me. Continue to abide in the shadow of My wings. Trust Me and our relationship to lead you into all truth.

The wisdom of the prudent is to give thought to their ways, but the folly of fools is deception.

—Proverbs 14:8

September 27

Dream again. Some of those dreams you dreamed long ago have been forgotten. I want you to take the time to remember those days when you would sit and dream about your future—the hope and dreams in your heart that brought joy. Dream again. Let Me bring back those memories when there was no pain, no hurt, no fear—nothing but joy and excitement about what the future might hold. I desire to make all your hopes and dreams come true. Take the time, reflect, and ask Me what you may.

There is surely a future hope for you, and your hope will not be cut off.

—Proverbs 23:18

September 28

Life isn't a race, it's a journey. Enjoy your journey. Stop and be grateful for what you have. Stop and smell the fresh air, see the sun shining, and hear the birds singing. I know life can get busy, running here and there with so much to do. But there is nothing more important than to stop, count your blessings, love those in your life, and dream about what will be. Running can cause you to get weary and miss out on so much. I never intended that My children would run to and fro searching for life. It's in the stillness where you can be refreshed and can breathe deeply.

I will refresh the weary and satisfy the faint.
—Jeremiah 31:25

September 29

Be patient with yourself. You have strengths but you also have weaknesses. That's OK. It's in your weakness that I AM strong. Do not get discouraged or despair about anything. As you travel through life, I AM right by your side. When you are faced with challenges, I AM your wisdom and strength. Do not let doubt or insecurity take over your thoughts. Keep your mind on Me and your heart on My love for you. Relax and be patient with yourself and others. My grace is sufficient to handle anything that comes your way.

But as for you, be strong and do not give up, for your work will be rewarded.
—2 Chronicles 15:7

September 30

Lay down your life for others. It isn't always easy but it is a life of fulfillment and it empowers you to hear more clearly from Me. The world says, "No, it's my way, the only way." My word to you is that it is always God's ways. When you lay down your motives, think of others, and are obedient to what I ask you to do, your life will be full and rewarding. It's not always easy and it's not always the most popular thing to do. But it is My way because it is what I call love.

This is how we know what love is: Jesus Christ laid down his life for us. And we ought to lay down our lives for our brothers.

—1 John 3:16

OCTOBER

October 1

ALWAYS LOOK FOR possibilities and opportunities. Even if the door looks closed, I can assure you there is another door that is open. Know that My desire for you is a life that is full and abundant in all good things. When you think all opportunities are gone, ask again. When you see with your natural eyes that all possibilities are depleted, look again. Remember, I AM the One who created the universe and everything in it. I AM the creator of all good things. Do not question My plans for you.

> Jesus replied, "What is impossible with men is possible with God."
>
> —Luke 18:27

October 2

When you are in pain and troubled, pour out your hurt to Me. Know that I will catch your tears and heal your hurts. It can be easy to just keep moving on without acknowledging pain, but those things that are not healed somehow always seem to come up again in the future. My children are broken and hurting, fearful and insecure, and need My healing touch. You may try and go to the world for healing, but it will not be long lasting. Come to Me, My child, and I will give you health and wholeness. I've given you all authority to trample on your enemies. Know this: My healing touch is final and lasts forever.

> "But for you who revere my name, the sun of righteousness will rise with healing in its wings. And you will go out and leap like calves released from the stall. Then you will trample down the wicked; they will be ashes under the soles of your feet on the day when I do these things," says the LORD Almighty.
> —Malachi 4:2–3

October 3

My Word is all you need today. There are many ways of communicating with others and ways to communicate with Me, but My Word is alive and living. It is for you yesterday, today, and tomorrow. It never changes. It becomes alive as you read and meditate on My truth to you. I want to speak to your heart and I want you to speak to mine. I AM so delighted when you spend time in My Word because it is My heart to you. Come close to me. Sit in that secret place where I can reveal My plans and purposes to you. It won't be a waste of time.

> However, as it is written: "No eye has seen, no ear has heard, no mind has conceived what God has prepared for those who love him"—but God has revealed it to us by his Spirit. The Spirit searches all things, even the deep things of God.
> —1 Corinthians 2:9–10

October 4

Your inheritance is in Me. Your identity is in Me. Your daily needs are with Me. A good father wants to pour out on his children. A good father wants to make sure his child is safe and secure. A good father wants to make sure the future is bright and fulfilling. All that your natural parents wanted to pour out on you, I desire to give you more and more. I want you to know you belong. You were predestined to be here and it was My greatest joy to see you born. As you were intricately designed by My hands, all that is before you is intricately designed as well. You are My happy thought and My heart's desire. I have many blessings for you, but you must know that you are My child to receive them. They are yours because of our relationship and not based on anything you would or wouldn't do. You are My child.

"My son," the father said, "you are always with me, and everything I have is yours."

—Luke 15:31

October 5

What is your passion? What is that creativity in you that sleeps? You were designed to be creative, but in that creativity you cannot look to the old ways. You must look for the new that releases the creativity. Many gifts and talents are given to you, so tap into that reservoir. New inventions, new solutions, and creative ideas come from tapping into the source from which all blessings flow. Stop and look at what you believe about the situation. Come and ask Me for the new way, new thought, new idea. I AM the Creator of all things and that creativity is yours. Let passion and desire arise. Release yourself into new creative avenues of promise.

See, the former things have taken place, and new things I declare; before they spring into being I announce them to you.

—Isaiah 42:9

October 6

Abandon yourself to Me completely. Do not worry about the cares of this world. It's the little worries that can cause your heart to be troubled. Put your complete trust in Me and surrender your anxious thoughts. I have not forgotten you and I have not forsaken you. Do not let one ounce of unbelief enter your heart. Unbelief will eat at your foundation and begin to bring instability in your life. Be careful. Be sensitive to My voice and My Spirit. Trusting Me in the good things is easy. Trusting Me when there is confusion and uncertainty is much more challenging. Come and lay down your concerns. Completely abandon and surrender all things to Me today.

> O Lord, you have searched me and you know me.
> You know when I sit and when I rise; you perceive
> my thoughts from afar. You discern my going out and
> my lying down; you are familiar with all my ways.
> —Psalm 139:1–3

October 7

Have fun today! Laugh and be merry. Let joy arise and be your strength this very moment. Before you became older in years, there were many days when you would play, laugh, giggle, and be carefree. As days have gone by, you have lost your sense of childlikeness. You have become too serious about your life and your relationships. I never intended for My children to be joyless and weary. It has always been My desire that they enjoy life and laughter. So laugh today. Let your joy bubble up. Let your light shine before others of the great joy within you.

> He redeemed my soul from going down to the pit,
> and I will live to enjoy the light.
>
> —Job 33:28

October 8

My grace is sufficient and can bring you contentment in all areas of your life. It's a divine exchange: you give Me your weakness and I give you My strength, sufficiency, and power. I will give you the compassion you need to help others. I AM in charge. Do not get bitter about your circumstances. Give them to Me and I will bring you wisdom. Don't worry about yesterday or tomorrow. Today is all you have, this very moment. Keep focused and watch Me move on your behalf.

> I am not saying this because I am in need, for I have learned to be content whatever the circumstances. I know what it is to be in need, and I know what it is to have plenty. I have learned the secret of being content in any and every situation, whether well fed or hungry, whether living in plenty or in want. I can do everything through him who gives me strength.
>
> —Philippians 4:11–13

October 9

Be intentional and rethink those things to which you feel obligated. Is it good or is it great or is it the greatest? Many times you have been involved with things that were good, but they weren't the best I have for you. Don't rely on yourself for wisdom. Be flexible and ready to make changes as I lead you. If you rely on your past to guide you, it will lead you in the wrong direction. If you count on the future for what you have need of today, it will bring disappointment. I want the best for you, My child. Your obedience is greater than your sacrifice. Rethink your choices.

> To do what is right and just is more acceptable to the LORD than sacrifice.
>
> —Proverbs 21:3

October 10

You have what you need and you will use it in this new season. There are new ways to make a difference and new ways to impact others. Do not be concerned if it looks different than you thought. I AM giving you greater authority in every area of your life. I AM giving you new vision and passion to accomplish more and more for My glory. There is greater grace to do what I have asked you to do. Be ready for what I have prepared for you. Spending time with Me and in My Word will equip you and train you to walk in confidence.

Experience My kingdom in a new, fresh way today. Rejoice because you have hope.

> I tell you the truth, anyone who has faith in me will do what I have been doing. He will do even greater things than these, because I am going to the Father.
>
> —John 14:12

October 11

Your eyes are the window to your soul. How is your soul affecting the way you see others? Make sure not to be wise in your own eyes. Do not be deceived by what you see. What do you think others might see through your eyes? Do they see hope, joy, thankfulness, faith, and a zeal for life? Or do they see hopelessness, discouragement, and death? Let My light shine through your eyes. Do not allow darkness to take up residence. Let My truth be revealed in your actions. What are others experiencing by being in a relationship with you? Life or death?

> If your eye is pure, there will be sunshine in your soul. But if your eye is clouded with evil thoughts and desires, you are in deep spiritual darkness. And oh, how deep that darkness can be!
>
> —Matthew 6:22 TLB

October 12

Do not look to the world for the things you need to know. It does not have the answers you are looking for. The world's mentality is focused on self—love of self, want of self, selfish actions, self-absorption, and how self-desires can be satisfied. Your old self was crucified with Me. It was corruptive and deceitful in its old ways. You put on the new man when the old nature died. Your nature was renewed with knowledge of Me and My ways. You know, My ways are so much higher than your ways. "Thy kingdom come, thy will be done on earth as it is heaven" is not about self. It's about My kingdom, power, and authority.

> For he has rescued us from the dominion of darkness and brought us into the kingdom of the Son he loves, in whom we have redemption, the forgiveness of sins.
>
> —Colossians 1:13–14

October 13

I AM found in the silence. I AM found in the stillness of your soul. It's not all about running around being busy doing this or doing that. Check your heart's motives and why you are involved in the things you are. Take time to sit at My feet and hear My voice, My counsel, and My heart for you and your circumstance. It is in the stillness that I can be heard. I want you to experience peace so you can be a peacemaker and serve others. Be still and know.

> The LORD will fight for you; you need only to be still.
> —Exodus 14:14

October 14

My Spirit will pour down like rain because I make all things new. Do not doubt this time you are in, this specific season, this exact time, this very moment. I AM in the rain and I AM in this time and place. Let Me pour Myself out in a fresh new way. Think of how the air smells and the clean fragrance after My rain has fallen. I can take things that appear to be dead and pour out a new, fresh rain that will bring life. Life will penetrate things of old, so do not despair the things of the past. I AM making all things new.

> Teach them the right way to live, and send rain on the land you gave your people for an inheritance.
> —2 Chronicles 6:27

October 15

My heart for you is to experience joy and freedom. I want to break off the chains and bondage that hold you back. Everything you have been through that has been hard and painful will not be wasted. Everything has added up to where you are right now and each moment, good or bad, had value. Let me restore the years the locust has eaten and return to you the joy and innocence. Everything will be used for My glory. Stand in awe of all that has been accomplished in your life through Me.

> Everyone was amazed and gave praise to God. They were filled with awe and said, "We have seen remarkable things today."
>
> —Luke 5:26

October 16

Draw near to Me and to My heart. I desire to give you breakthrough in this time of turmoil. Come experience My peace. It's the little foxes, the little stones, and the little lies that can turn things upside down. Keep your focus on Me and My Word in your life. Let My holiness fill you to overflowing. I AM faithful and I promise to be faithful to My Word. Just as a butterfly is surrounded in a safe cocoon, I want to be that safe place for you. I want you to know My peace and gain strength in these times of weakness. Trust Me for whatever you need today.

> The former regulation is set aside because it was weak and useless (for the law made nothing perfect), and a better hope is introduced, by which we draw near to God.
>
> —Hebrews 7:18–19

October 17

You must go against the grain to leave a legacy. You must trust in Me and have courage to fulfill My destiny in you. You are different and unique. You are strong and courageous in all your ways. I AM giving you new ideas, new ventures, new relationships, and new thoughts about how you see yourself and others. You are unique to this world. The world needs what you have, so you must surrender all insecurity to Me. You must be willing to go where no one else has gone. You are a pioneer who plows into new territories because of your uniqueness. Plowing is hard; plotting through hard ground is laborious, so stay strong and do not get weary. I AM with you at all times.

> Teach me to do your will, for you are my God; may your good Spirit lead me on level ground.
>
> —Psalm 143:10

October 18

Inspire others through your story. Don't complain about your circumstances, but know that you are blessed to have the opportunity to inspire others. Don't try to be anybody else other than who I created. Don't feel defeated because of your seeming weakness, but know that I empower you to do great things. Struggles will come and go, but they do not need to stop you in your tracks. My presence will provide all you need. Do not limit Me and do not limit yourself. Do not let that victim mentality have a hold on your mind or your thoughts. You are not a victim; you are more than a conqueror in Me.

> I know that everything God does will endure forever; nothing can be added to it and nothing taken from it. God does it so that men will revere him.
>
> —Ecclesiastes 3:14

October 19

Be strong and courageous in these times. Do not faint or get weary. For I AM a God of miracles and I want to perform miracles in your life, your relationships, your job, your family, and your health. You have depended on others for that special word, encouragement, and good report, but you must come to Me. I AM the Way, the Truth, and the Life, and I will make sure your life is full of promise and joy. Do not get discouraged or disheartened, for the story of your life is still being written. Rest assured that I know the end of the story. Be strong in Me alone.

> Again the one who looked like a man touched me and gave me strength. "Do not be afraid, O man highly esteemed," he said. "Peace! Be strong now; be strong."
>
> —Daniel 10:18–19

October 20

Your soul is thirty and dry. Your emotions are up and down. Your mind is at times confused and doubtful about what you see. Decisions are hard and you sometimes feel frozen in how you might respond. I want you to hunger and thirst for Me. Where there is a place of weariness and dryness, I AM your fresh drink of water. Do not think that I ever get tired of pouring out My love and Spirit on you. I AM the One who can bring the refreshing you need and the refreshing for which you cry out. Much fruit comes from sun and water. Let Me be your only Son and bring a refreshing to you today.

> O God, you are my God, earnestly I seek you; my soul thirsts for you, my body longs for you, in a dry and weary land where there is no water.
>
> —Psalm 63:1

October 21

Time is spacious and long. Relax and rest—I don't want you to rush. Enjoy the time I have given you and enjoy My timing in your life. This specific time will be your worship and bring Me joy. Through that joy you will experience strength. Don't only look at your feet, but look as far as your eyes can see. My universe is massive and most of it is unexplored, so let Me show you little by little, step by step, moment by moment. Let go of what is behind and look forward to what I have in store for you. Enjoy the ride. Hold on, because it will be the ride of your life. Have fun, laugh, and be encouraged.

> Now faith is being sure of what we hope for and certain of what we do not see. This is what the ancients were commended for. By faith we understand that the universe was formed at God's command, so that what is seen was not made out of what was visible.
>
> —Hebrews 11:1–3

October 22

Do not be afraid of what I want to show you in your life. I want to reveal to you those secret things, those things that are hidden away and in darkness, those things that are holding your emotions locked up. I only bring these things to you for the purpose of healing. Many hurtful things have happened in your life that you don't understand. Do not despair, do not give up, and do not be afraid. Fear is your greatest enemy, but faith is what is required in this time. The more you surrender yourself to Me, the more relaxed and safe you are. My guidance in your journey will bring you safety, protection, and intimacy. That is what you have always wanted, that is what you have cried out for, and I too want you to walk in complete freedom. Trust this process and let Me bring the healing required.

Then your light will break forth like the dawn, and your healing will quickly appear; then your righteousness will go before you, and the glory of the LORD will be your rear guard. Then you will call, and the LORD will answer; you will cry for help, and he will say: Here am I.

—Isaiah 58:8–9

October 23

I AM a city of refuge for you. I AM your hiding place. Life can be hard and fearful, but know that you always have a place to come. When disappointment or discouragement comes your way, know you can come to Me for comfort. When insecurity and unworthiness want to cast you down and make you feel insignificant, look up to Me and find your hiding place in Me. My arms are always open to you. My ears are always ready to listen. My heart will always be open to you. I AM a place that will be secure, strong, and everlasting. I AM a shelter and your hope both in times of trial and in times of rest.

Guard my life and rescue me; let me not be put to shame, for I take refuge in you.

—Psalm 25:20

October 24

Be in unity with all people. Do not be an instrument used in the enemy's hands to bring disunity or pain. Come to Me and ask for the wisdom you need to bring hope and reconciliation. Relationships can be difficult and hard at times, but in the midst of that difficulty, I want love to flow. Love is the act of forgiveness and the desire to give rather than receive. Love lays down a life for the other. Just as I freely have given you love, I want you to freely give it away. Unity can be a powerful instrument in your hands to bring change. Unity is walking in maturity. Unity will heal. Always choose unity.

> Make every effort to keep the unity of the Spirit through the bond of peace.
>
> —Ephesians 4:3

October 25

I have given you all authority to live your life to the fullest. You don't fight against humanity, flesh, and blood, but against spiritual darkness and powers. Authority has been given to you so you can overcome all obstacles in your life. Submit to My authority in every situation. Through that authority you will be given the responsibility and power to walk in total freedom. Be strong and courageous, knowing I AM all you need in everything.

For in Christ all the fullness of the Deity lives in bodily form, and you have been given fullness in Christ, who is the head over every power and authority.

—Colossians 2:9–10

October 26

You belong. You were predestined to be here for such a time as this. I knitted you in your mother's womb and desired that you be born. My DNA is in your DNA. Nothing you can do can change that DNA. You are Mine and I AM yours. Your inheritance is secure in Me and My desire is to lavish you with all the love I have. An inheritance is a gift and not based on anything you will or will not do. It is an unconditional gift from Me that I give to all My children. Receive it freely.

For the LORD will not reject his people; he will never forsake his inheritance.

—Psalm 94:14

October 27

Do not think you have to perform. Performance brings fear and anxiety and pressure that are not necessary. You do not have to cover yourself in shame or fear. You do not need to worry what man may think of you. I want you to rest, knowing you are giving your best in all situations. Rest, knowing you have been created in My image. Do not run here and there, trying to please others. Be assured of My love for you in all situations and with all people. I will be with You wherever you go.

> The LORD replied, "My Presence will go with you, and I will give you rest."
>
> —Exodus 33:14

October 28

Cross over. Cross over from famine to plenty. Cross over from sorrow to joy. Cross over from lack to plenty. Cross over from insecurity to security in Me. Cross over to your promised land. Even though you don't see all you need to see, trust Me to give you only the best. I may not always tell you what lies ahead, but you can know I have your best interests in My heart. You will not lack anything. Trust Me and walk with boldness and courage.

> But you will cross the Jordan and settle in the land the LORD your God is giving you as an inheritance, and he will give you rest from all your enemies around you so that you will live in safety.
>
> —Deuteronomy 12:10

October 29

Abide in Me. Take up residence in My presence. Wait and be still. My presence will be all you need today and in the coming days ahead. My presence will chase away the lies and will only allow truth to prevail. I AM your hiding place. Take shelter in My heavenly dwelling. Be strong, knowing My love dwells in you. Let your joy in Me overflow to a hopeless world. Let My life take residence in your life so all that remains is My love.

> Remain in me, and I will remain in you. No branch can bear fruit by itself; it must remain in the vine. Neither can you bear fruit unless you remain in me.
> —John 15:40

October 30

Persevere through all your trials. Do not keep your eyes on the troubles, but keep your eyes on the promises I have spoken to you. Stand firm and steadfast. Do not waver to the left or to the right. Do not surrender to your emotions, because they change from day to day. Persevere through all things with strength and encouragement. It will build faith and it will build character. When all is said and done and you look back over your life, you will see how I have given you the strength to persevere. You will be amazed at My enduring mercy, compassion, and faithfulness to you.

As you know, we consider blessed those who have persevered. You have heard of Job's perseverance and have seen what the LORD finally brought about. The LORD is full of compassion and mercy.

—James 5:11

October 31

You are My beloved, My friend, and My treasure. I desire to see you sparkle and shine like a diamond, with all its facets ignited and illuminated by My love. You are precious to Me. Do not shrink back from who I have created you to be. My design for you is great and magnificent, and your true destiny is always in Me. I love you for all you are. Even in your weakest moments I stand beside you as the mighty lion, loyal and fiercely protective of your delicate heart. My love makes you strong, beloved. Believe in all you are and all I AM in you.

The LORD is my strength and my shield; my heart trusts in him, and I am helped. My heart leaps for joy and I will give thanks to him in song.

—Psalm 28:7

NOVEMBER

November 1

COURAGE. CLIMB UP the mountain with Me, My beloved. Have courage, do not fear, the slope will not be slippery as I AM climbing with you. My hand holds your hand, My feet guide your feet, and My eyes are your eyes. I will raise you up above the nations, above the things of this world, and show you the love I have for My people. Do not be afraid—take courage. I AM your way. I AM your light. Be bold and climb the mountain, My beloved.

> Many peoples will come and say, "Come, let us go up to the mountain of the LORD, to the house of the God of Jacob. He will teach us his ways, so that we may walk in his paths."
>
> —Isaiah 2:3

November 2

Walk with Me, My child. I AM your Father and I love you so. Fear not, for in Me there is no fear. Fear will always try to separate you from Me, but always know that I AM more powerful than fear. I AM the creator of all things and all things submit to Me. You will never have need of fear in your life when you walk with Me. Remember, it's My perfect love that casts out all fear. My love is all you will ever need. I defeated fear at the cross—for you!

> But now, this is what the LORD says—he who created you, O Jacob, he who formed you, O Israel: "Fear not, for I have redeemed you; I have summoned you by name; you are mine. When you pass through the waters, I will be with you; and when you pass through the rivers, they will not sweep over you. When you walk through the fire, you will not be burned; the flames will not set you ablaze."
>
> —Isaiah 43:1–2

November 3

I AM the fountain of life. When all has passed away and there is nothing left, I will still BE. If you come to Me and drink, you will be sustained. If you come to Me and drink, you will find that in the end you will still remain, for I AM in those who are in Me. For where My water is, there is life. Without Me there is only death, but from Me pour rivers of living water. Drink, drink, drink from the fountain.

He said to me: "It is done. I am the Alpha and the Omega, the Beginning and the End. To him who is thirsty I will give to drink without cost from the spring of the water of life."

—Revelation 21:6

November 4

At times you feel your sense of inadequacy or lack of training disqualifies you from serving others. That is not true. In fact, it is your inadequacy that qualifies you. It keeps you pliable, humble, and always depending on Me for your wisdom, understanding, strength, and power. The world may say, "You are inadequate," but I say, "You are more than adequate in My kingdom." I qualify the called. Rest, knowing that you have all you need. All you have to do is cry out and ask for My help. I AM all you need. Stay humble and in My presence. I will show you glorious things to come!

And those he predestined, he also called; those he called, he also justified; those he justified, he also glorified.

—Romans 8:30

November 5

Give your hurts and feelings of revenge or retaliation to Me today. Things have been hurtful and your immediate response is to hurt others, but that is not My way. Give those hurts and disappointments to Me first and let Me bring the needed healing. I will heal those hurts and give you the wisdom and instruction you need to handle the situation. Hurts happen in life. When you are hurt, the only one who can heal you is Me. Do not hurt others out of your own hurt. It's not always easy, I know.

> Do not take revenge, my friends, but leave room for God's wrath, for it is written: "It is mine to avenge; I will repay," says the LORD.
>
> —Romans 12:19

November 6

I will never leave you or abandon you. There have been times when you have wondered and questioned whether I was present in a certain situation. I want you to know that even if you didn't see Me, I have always been with you and will continue to be by your side. When you lost your way, it was I who guided you back on the path. When you felt alone and lonely, I was there to bring comfort. When you were blind and could not see, I helped you find the truth along the way and we walked side by side. My promise to you is that I AM by your side at all times. I AM a God who is big enough for anything that comes your way. Rely on and trust in Me.

> Because of your great compassion you did not abandon them in the desert. By day the pillar of cloud did not cease to guide them on their path, nor the pillar of fire by night to shine on the way they were to take.
>
> —Nehemiah 9:19

November 7

Do not rely on any crutches in your life. My will and purposes will be revealed in your life as you walk with Me. As you look back on this time, you will be thankful for the rest and peace you gained as you put your trust in Me. Leaning on a crutch will only delay My purposes because you must learn to put your trust in Me. It is very difficult to teach and instruct you if you are relying on anything other than Me. Even if you walk with a limp, you will walk completely under My power and authority. Rely on My strength.

> Surely God is my salvation; I will trust and not be afraid. The LORD, the LORD, is my strength and my song; he has become my salvation.
>
> —Isaiah 12:2

November 8

Dance, My beloved. Dance with Me, let Me spin you and hold you as your beauty radiates for all the world to see. I created you to be an incarnation of beauty, of strength, to represent the glory of who I AM in you. As you dance, all the worries and hurts will fly away. As you continue to dance and embrace the loveliness of who I AM in you, new desires and memories will be created in your heart and mind. My joy is your strength as you sail across the dance floor with Me. Will you dance with Me?

> Then maidens will dance and be glad, young men and old as well. I will turn their mourning into gladness; I will give them comfort and joy instead of sorrow.
>
> —Jeremiah 31:13

November 9

I want to change your mindset in the way you see your life. I want to renew your mind and bring clarity into your belief system so you will know My truth. When others have hurt you or spoken hurtful words to you, they can penetrate your heart to cause you to look at the world and Me in an ungodly way. I want to restore your soul and renew your mind so your thoughts are on My Word and My truth and not based on what others have said. Your destiny in part is based on what you believe about yourself and the world around you. When your thoughts are on Me, your destiny is in alignment with My purposes.

A simple man believes anything, but a prudent man gives thought to his steps.

—Proverbs 14:15

November 10

Check your heart today. Any place where you are hurt or feel like you have judged others, you must repent quickly. When there is judgment in your heart, that judgment you use on others will come back on you. It is a spiritual law. Do not criticize or grumble with others, as it is an open door to oppression in your life. Many of My precious children do not know or see that their heart issues stop them from receiving the love and affection they so desire, especially from their loved ones. Release your hurt and judgments to Me and be free.

For in the same way you judge others, you will be judged, and with the measure you use, it will be measured to you.

—Matthew 7:2

November 11

You are anointed with the Holy Spirit. I have anointed you to do great things. My anointing has been poured out on you to move in power and authority. My anointing breaks any yoke of bondage. My anointing covers you and everything you do. My anointing removes burdens and anything that would bring destruction in your life. I AM the anointed One and you are in Me. I have passed My anointing on to you to do greater things than I have. Freely receive My anointing today.

> And it shall come to pass in that day, that his burden shall be taken away from off thy shoulder, and his yoke from off thy neck, and the yoke shall be destroyed because of the anointing.
>
> —Isaiah 10:27 KJV

November 12

My joy in you is complete. Be joyful at all times. Laugh much and know My joy. Laughter will heal your soul. It gives Me great joy to see you prosper and to fill you with abundant joy. Sing and dance with joy. Know that strength will come from joy. Peace will happen in your life as you live with an attitude of gratitude, thankfulness, and joy. Even in the hard days you can experience great joy in the midst of the trial. Walk in joy unspeakable and full of glory. Prosperity will come.

> He will yet fill your mouth with laughter and your lips with shouts of joy.
>
> —Job 8:21

November 13

Many obstacles may try and get in the way of progress. Life is full of obstacles. Some are larger than others and some are insignificant, but yet they are obstacles just the same. You are in the valley of decision every time an obstacle comes your way. Which way will you choose? One of life or one of death? One of hope or one of despair? It's your choice. My Word is full of promises and a future with a hope for you that you can always choose. The enemy has his own plan, which is to kill, steal, and destroy. I have given you the will to choose. Choose wisely.

For the creation was subjected to frustration, not by its own choice, but by the will of the one who subjected it, in hope that the creation itself will be liberated from its bondage to decay and brought into the glorious freedom of the children of God.
—Romans 8:20–21

November 14

May faith arise in you today. Your faith will continue to grow the more you exercise your willingness to obey. Obedience opens the door to faith and faith opens the door to the miraculous. Let Me show you miraculous power today. Know that when your faith begins to grow, you are moving out of unbelief into the realm of strong belief in Me. So choose to exercise more faith in the small things so I can begin to show you the miraculous things. Faith and works go hand in hand, work together, and complete My purpose. I can't do it without your faith.

> Was not our ancestor Abraham considered righteous for what he did when he offered his son Isaac on the altar? You see that his faith and his actions were working together, and his faith was made complete by what he did.
>
> —James 2:21–22

November 15

Tears are cleansing. Tears wash away the hurt and pain. I catch every one of your tears in My bottle. The world says, "You are weak if you cry," but I say, "You are strong because you cry." Hurts can get so bottled up over the years that you might be afraid to let those tears flow. But I say to you, "My beloved, those who sow in tears will reap in joy. I AM here to comfort you and restore you. I have heard your prayers, I have seen your tears, and I will heal you. So let them flow freely and without restraint. I will continue to heal your heart as you release the hurts." That is My promise to you always.

> You number my wanderings; put my tears into Your bottle; are they not in Your book? When I cry out to You, then my enemies will turn back; this I know, because God is for me.
>
> —Psalm 56:8–9 NKJV

November 16

My hand is upon you for good. Through My Son I have paid the cost of all your sin and My plan is that you will live a life in freedom and understand My grace. It is through My grace that you begin to accept who you are and allow Me to take the heavy yoke with which you burden yourself. Acceptance is not meant to be a joyful moment filled with warm fuzzy feelings. Instead, acceptance is a moment where you see yourself for who I created you to be and understand that My grace covers the sinful life you have lived. No sin is too great for Me to forgive or to keep Me away from you. Accept My love, My precious child, and begin a journey of acceptance today.

> Let us then approach the throne of grace with confidence, so that we may receive mercy and find grace to help us in our time of need.
> —Hebrews 4:16

November 17

When I went into the temple and found so many things there that did not honor Me, I became angry and turned over the tables. I AM jealous for you, for you are My temple. When I find things in you that take you away from My love, I become angry—never at you, never at the temple, only angry with that which has taken you from Me. When I come into My temple I will clean it out with a fire so hot it will leave nothing behind. It is a purifying fire; it is My purifying love.

> And what union can there be between God's temple and idols? For you are God's temple, the home of the living God, and God has said of you, "I will live in them and walk among them, and I will be their God and they shall be my people."
>
> —2 Corinthians 6:16

November 18

Hope deferred makes the heart sick. Hope fades and discouragement comes. Disappointments happen and your heart sinks into despair. Things can look very dark and you feel that change is impossible. Lies come and you can't even see the truth. Darkness comes in and you see no light. I understand. I hear the pain. I AM not far away. Trust, and open your heart to Me once again and let Me bring the healing. Love is what you desire and love is what I AM. Love is what I want to pour into you to heal the wounds. Trust again and I will heal your heart. Know that the enemy is the father of lies—do not fall for his lies.

> See to it, brothers, that none of you has a sinful, unbelieving heart that turns away from the living God. But encourage one another daily, as long as it is called Today, so that none of you may be hardened by sin's deceitfulness.
>
> —Hebrews 3:12–13

November 19

Your deliverance is at hand. I AM your great Deliverer. I AM the Repairer of the Breach. I AM your Healer. I AM your Comforter. I AM that I AM. I AM all you need. You can do everything with My help, knowing I AM the great I AM. What else do you need? Nothing can satisfy and nothing can bring the healing and joy I can bring. Material possessions or earthly relationships cannot be as fulfilling as Me and My love for you. Rely on Me and trust the truth of My Word. Walk into your promised land and possess your purpose and destiny!

> My heart rejoices in the LORD; in the LORD my horn is lifted high. My mouth boasts over my enemies, for I delight in your deliverance.
>
> —1 Samuel 2:1

November 20

Kindness and faithfulness go hand in hand. Show kindness wherever you go. Reveal your faithfulness in Me and My faithfulness in you. Many in your community of friends are watching and benefiting from your kindness. They see My hand working in your life. They are surprised by your kindness to others. You are very unique in a world that is focused on self and selfishness. Give to others? Most people do not understand the heart of giving as you do. You give from a heart of kindness that comes deep from our relationship. Continue to pour out acts of kindness as I direct you. The more you pour out, the more you receive.

> I led them with cords of human kindness, with ties of love; I lifted the yoke from their neck and bent down to feed them.
>
> —Hosea 11:4

November 21

Look into the mirror, My beloved. What do you see? What do you hear? What do you believe? Who do you think you are? Do you believe what man says about you or do you believe what I say or what My Word says about you? Are you full of faith or doubtful about your identity? Are you unsure of the plans I have for you? Do you waver back and forth between the old nature and the new creation? That is absolutely normal. Do not condemn yourself, because I do not condemn you. You are on the path of healing, and each day you get the opportunity to know Me and My love in a greater and greater degree. Never give up and never doubt My love. One day you will look in the mirror and see My image.

> Do not lie to each other, since you have taken off your old self with its practices and have put on the new self, which is being renewed in knowledge in the image of its Creator.
>
> —Colossians 3:9–10

November 22

The battle is not yours, it is Mine. Go in the name of the Lord in all your conflicts and know that the battle has already been won. You are more than a conqueror, and with Me all victory is yours. I have given you all power and authority to walk in total freedom, so there is no need to fear or doubt. Conflicts and battles are a part of life, but there is no need for you to feel inferior or insecure about the outcome. You are armed, so fight the good fight of faith, with assurance. I have enlisted you in My army and you are prepared to win. I AM with you.

> You armed me with strength for battle; you made my adversaries bow at my feet. You made my enemies turn their backs in flight, and I destroyed my foes.
> —2 Samuel 22:40–41

November 23

Do not let offense enter your heart. It is the very thing that will give the enemy access to your soul. Expectations and putting pressure on others will always set you up for disappointment and discouragement. Once the enemy has the open door to hurt or wound your heart, he takes advantage of the situation to bring more and more oppression. Keep your heart open, soft, and pliable, but keep it guarded from the enemy's weapons. Do not let hardness enter your heart. It is always wise to overlook the offense and stay in forgiveness and love.

He who covers over an offense promotes love, but whoever repeats the matter separates close friends.

—Proverbs 17:9

November 24

Your chains are broken. Ties to your hurt and hurts from the past are broken. I accomplished all of that at the cross for you. The truth is that you are free and have always been free since I died on the cross and rose again. All freedom was accomplished through My death and resurrection. I want you to know that you are loved, cherished, valued, treasured, and worthy of My love. All that I did, I did it just for you so you may know what true love is. Be free, My precious child!

It is for freedom that Christ has set us free. Stand firm, then, and do not let yourselves be burdened again by a yoke of slavery.

—Galatians 5:1

November 25

Cherish every moment you have, love with your whole heart, and live fearlessly. Trust My timing even when you are anxious, and keep your heart and mind on Me. Every breath you take and every moment you are awake, give Me praise. Praise and worship are weapons of warfare. I inhabit the praises of My people and I will inhabit your circumstances. I so want you to dwell in My presence and know that your life is rich and full. Hold Me in your heart and cherish these moments we have. It will be like drinking a glass of cold water when you are in a dry and thirsty place.

> Forget the former things; do not dwell on the past. See, I am doing a new thing! Now it springs up; do you not perceive it? I am making a way in the desert and streams in the wasteland.
>
> —Isaiah 43:18–19

November 26

Perspective. Passion. Purpose. You have been given these gifts—not for you alone but for those you impact. Know that your perspective can change if you choose to meditate on Me and My Word. Passion can be ignited in you to live your life to the fullest and let the fire burn inside your soul. Purpose is your journey. It is not the final destination but the journey along the way. Many people are focused on themselves and their problems, but I want you to focus on Me and My life, which will bring abundant life to you and to others. Trust that I order your steps.

> A man's steps are directed by the LORD. How then can anyone understand his own way?
>
> —Proverbs 20:24

November 27

I AM. Everywhere you are and everywhere you go, I AM. Make a decision today to push toward your destiny by hearing My Word and obeying what I say to you. I AM all you need. There are many directions you can take, many roads to travel, but the only one and sure way is to follow Me. All instructions for life are hidden in My Word. The more you enter into My presence and hear My words for you, the more you will experience peace, joy, and hope. Be grafted in Me and let Me be your source of life so you can prosper.

> Whoever gives heed to instruction prospers, and blessed is he who trusts in the LORD.
> —Proverbs 16:20

November 28

I AM full of grace and compassion. I AM faithful and just. I AM wise and steadfast. I AM so much more than the world. Amazingly, I have molded you into My image so there are no flaws. Whatever needs you have and whatever struggles you are walking through today, know you can call on Me any time. Let Me build a strong foundation in you so your roots will go deep. There is so much more I want you to know about Me, but it takes time and commitment on your part. I AM a living Word to you, and I want you to know My heart for you and your loved ones. Beloved, come and spend time with Me today.

Teach me knowledge and good judgment, for I believe in your commands. Before I was afflicted I went astray, but now I obey your word. You are good, and what you do is good; teach me your decrees.
—Psalm 119:66–68

November 29

Be happy no matter where you are. Everything you have walked through has been preparation. Know that it takes time to build a character that is strong and stable. You have many gifts and talents, but it is your character that will take precedence over any job, ministry, or friendship. Do not despise the correction or instruction from Me that will strengthen your foundation and bring healing. Everything I do and everything I ask you to do is for a purpose. Trust in the course corrections. You have come a long way and I AM so proud of you.

Listen to my instruction and be wise; do not ignore it.
—Proverbs 8:33

November 30

Rest in the midst of your busyness. Take time to be with Me and let Me refresh your soul. Many things need to be done, but the most important is keeping your eyes focused on Me. Man has his traditions and expectations, but the only desire I have is for us to know each other.

It is in the stillness, the restful place, that you will be able to hear Me clearly. Rest like still water that has no agenda other than to be still. The conditions of your family, health, and sense of well-being are based on how much peace and rest you have. Let Me fill you up where you are dry and give you peace where you are troubled. Come rest in My arms today, knowing everything will be accomplished that needs to be accomplished.

> Then, because so many people were coming and going that they did not even have a chance to eat, he said to them, "Come with me by yourselves to a quiet place and get some rest."
>
> —Mark 6:31

DECEMBER

December 1

DO NOT MAKE decisions based on your feelings. Feelings are fickle and are not always based on truth. Feelings are good and healthy as a way to communicate with Me and others, but they are not always based on My truth on the matter. Express your feelings freely and be real with Me. Get in touch with what your feelings are wanting to say, but do not make major decisions based on those feelings. My Word, My truth, My heart, and My love will always override your feelings.

> Why are you downcast, O my soul? Why so disturbed within me? Put your hope in God, for I will yet praise him, my Savior and my God.
> —Psalm 42:11

December 2

Choices. So many choices. You can walk around a grocery store and be inundated with choices—some good and some not so good. There are so many items to choose from, it can be overwhelming! I want you to know that it was My choice and only choice to come and give you life. I had no other choice to make. Because of that, I knew My purpose, and even when I didn't know the plan, I knew My destiny would be fulfilled and you would be free from sin and death. Choose life today. Choose those things that are good for you. Don't be tempted to choose as the world chooses.

> You did not choose me, but I chose you and appointed you to go and bear fruit—fruit that will last. Then the Father will give you whatever you ask in my name.
> —John 15:16

December 3

Change the filter through which you see your life. Filters can cause you to perceive things in life that are either clouded or untrue. In your mind you can say, "No, that is exactly what is happening," but the truth may be hidden because of the filter. A filter in a furnace collects dirt and waste products, but if not changed, it can cause the heating system to become clogged and eventually shut down. It's the same thing with filters you have constructed in your mind. Revisit those places that seem to keep you shut down or ineffective. It may just be that the filter needs to be replaced by My truth and My heart for you. I want to bring healing to all areas of your life.

> Jesus stopped and said, "Call him." So they called to the blind man, "Cheer up! On your feet! He's calling you." Throwing his cloak aside, he jumped to his feet and came to Jesus. "What do you want me to do for you?" Jesus asked him. The blind man said, "Rabbi, I want to see." "Go," said Jesus, "your faith has healed you." Immediately he received his sight and followed Jesus along the road.
>
> —Mark 10:49–52

December 4

My beloved. My precious one. Today is the greatest day of My life. I get to spend it with you. I get to hear your voice, listen to your concerns, and encourage you. That is just what I want to do as your Father. I want you to know you belong. I want you to know you are valued and precious to Me. I love you and cherish our times together. You are the greatest gift to Me. I want to hold you, speak to your heart, and guide you along the way. Your purpose and destiny are secure in Me.

> You hear, O LORD, the desire of the afflicted; you encourage them, and you listen to their cry, defending the fatherless and the oppressed, in order that man, who is of the earth, may terrify no more.
>
> —Psalm 10:17–18

December 5

Let Me feed your spirit. Let Me provide all the needs you have. Just as a momma bird feeds her little ones, I want to be your provider. I know your needs and exactly how to meet those needs. So come and eat all you want. There are many things I want to share with you about who I AM, My heart, and all My ways that will direct your paths. The desire to eat has to come from you. When you are hungry and thirsty for more, I will be your nourishment. You will grow strong and steady. Your spiritual health is just as important as your physical and mental health. Do not delay—your whole life depends on it.

> They all ate the same spiritual food and drank the same spiritual drink; for they drank from the spiritual rock that accompanied them, and that rock was Christ.
>
> —1 Corinthians 10:3–4

December 6

What seems to be blocking you? At times, you look around and see others' faults and question their motives while at the same time you have a plank in your own eye. It doesn't mean you don't love Me or have no desire to do My will. It just means there is a place of deception, a place in your heart you cannot see. You see life through disappointments and rejection. You haven't felt loved or honored, so you have limited the way others see you and how you see others. Let Me take off the blinders. Let Me remove the plank in your eye so you can see clearly. Will you allow Me?

> Why do you look at the speck of sawdust in your brother's eye and pay no attention to the plank in your own eye?
>
> —Matthew 7:3

December 7

Your treasure in heaven is guaranteed. There is no one or no way that any of that treasure can be stolen or taken away from you. You have persevered. You have believed in Me and believed in the process of refining what I have accomplished in your life. You never gave up or quit. Do not fear what your future will be. You are secure in Me. Whatever you have or desire to hold on to, surrender it all to Me.

> Sell your possessions and give to the poor. Provide purses for yourselves that will not wear out, a treasure in heaven that will not be exhausted, where no thief comes near and no moth destroys. For where your treasure is, there your heart will be also.
>
> —Luke 12:33–34

December 8

Stir up the gifts within you. Exercise those gifts and grow. My gifts to you are irrevocable. Fan the flame that lives within you and build My church. Build the people of My church. Train and equip all those with whom you come in contact to exercise the gifts I have given them. Everyone has been given a measure of faith, so use your faith in the building process. The flame must continue to burn without fear because I have given you all power and love. Let those gifts come forth to touch a dying world. I want to use you as My special ambassador.

> So it is with you. Since you are eager to have spiritual gifts, try to excel in gifts that build up the church.
>
> —1 Corinthians 14:12

December 9

What do you see when you watch others? How can you determine whether someone knows Me or not? Do you really know the issues of a person's heart just by his or her appearance? Be careful not to put anyone in a box. Tradition and laws can cause your heart to judge. I want you to see out of My eyes. I want you to discern out of My heart. I want you to hear what is not being said rather than what you hear. Walking with Me will be your assurance that I AM leading you and instructing you. Let My heart be in you, My child. It is a heart that is soft and pliable before Me.

> See to it that no one takes you captive through hollow and deceptive philosophy, which depends on human tradition and the basic principles of this world, rather than on Christ.
>
> —Colossians 2:8

December 10

My supply is limitless. There are no caps or limits. Whatever you believe in will be yours. It takes faith, courage, wisdom, understanding, and revelation of My ways. I desire to give you the kingdom and all that pertains to that kingdom, but you must first stop limiting Me and limiting yourself. There are many treasures that are yours if only you would believe. There are dreams yet to be fulfilled if only you would trust Me. There are hidden treasures in the suffering if only you would look. There is nothing that will stop the flow of My love for you. My love never fails. My supply never runs dry.

> Now he who supplies seed to the sower and bread for food will also supply and increase your store of seed and will enlarge the harvest of your righteousness. You will be made rich in every way so that you can be generous on every occasion, and through us your generosity will result in thanksgiving to God.
>
> —2 Corinthians 9:10–11

December 11

Laugh and be joyous today. Look for things to laugh about. Enjoy your life and make sure those around you see your joy—not joy or happiness in the worldly sense but joy in your relationship with Me and My relationship with you. We make great partners. So laugh! Take off all the burdens and give them to Me today. Be like a child and let loose.

> There is a time for everything, and a season for every activity under heaven … a time to weep and a time to laugh, a time to mourn and a time to dance.
> —Ecclesiastes 3:1, 4

December 12

Persevere through the hard times. Strength and hope are developed as you walk day by day through the hills and valleys of life. My strength is yours when you feel weak. The road is narrow because it keeps you within My reach. When you try to walk outside the boundaries I have set for you, life becomes hard and difficult. But also when I AM pruning and shaping you into My image, those times can feel just as hard. So be encouraged and keep your hope alive. You are strong and mighty in Me no matter the times.

No discipline seems pleasant at the time, but painful. Later on, however, it produces a harvest of righteousness and peace for those who have been trained by it.

—Hebrews 12:11

December 13

Yes, you have failed at times, but My mercy covers it. I have mercy on whom I want to pour My mercy on, and that is you. I AM rich in mercy because I love you so much. Just as you have received mercy, give mercy away. Do not hold a grudge or offense in your heart. Stay in a place of forgiveness and be merciful. Remember, blessed are those who are merciful, as they will be shown mercy.

But go and learn what this means: "I desire mercy, not sacrifice." For I have not come to call the righteous, but sinners.

—Matthew 9:13

December 14

Let Me inspire and encourage you to a greater place in Me. Stop at the fountain and get a refreshing drink for the journey. Fill up with mercy, grace, gratitude, joy, peace, and love. Remember, My love covers a multitude of sins. Keep your heart and mind pure. Let

My water cleanse you and purify your thoughts. You can't finish the race dehydrated and in a daze. You must run and finish the race with all power and authority, alive and well.

> Therefore, since we are surrounded by such a great cloud of witnesses, let us throw off everything that hinders and the sin that so easily entangles, and let us run with perseverance the race marked out for us.
>
> —Hebrews 12:1

December 15

I AM your refuge and place of safety. Sit under My everlasting arms and let Me cover you under the shadow of My wings. All you need will be met in the presence of My love. There are enemies after your salvation and peace. There are trials and tribulations that will cause you to faint. But My ways are always perfect. I will be your shield from the enemy's fiery darts. I AM your safe place to fall. Come and put your trust in Me.

> The LORD is a refuge for the oppressed, a stronghold in times of trouble. Those who know your name will trust in you, for you, LORD, have never forsaken those who seek you.
>
> —Psalm 9:9–10

December 16

Come into that secret place with Me. There are so many mysteries I want to reveal to you. Spend time with Me so you know and understand the times in which you are living. Your current situations can only be discerned through My Spirit and My heart. Man can try to figure out things through humanness, but it is I who hold the truth. It is I who will give you knowledge and wisdom. Seek Me and you will find Me. Let My truth prevail and call on My name.

> From now on I will tell you of new things, of hidden things unknown to you. They are created now, and not long ago; you have not heard of them before today.
> —Isaiah 48:6–7

December 17

Think of your highest joys and your lowest sorrows. What have you concluded about Me? Has this journey been one lived in faith or has it been one lived unbelieving? Mountains high and valleys low—they all have had a purpose. When you climbed those mountains, the views were exquisite and breathtaking. But when you were in the valleys, you felt closed in and your vision seemed to be impaired. Remember the many lessons you have learned as you have walked step by step with Me. In those places where you felt weak, I was your strength; and in those places where you were strong, I was your greatest cheerleader.

You will go out in joy and be led forth in peace; the mountains and hills will burst into song before you, and all the trees of the field will clap their hands.

—Isaiah 55:12

December 18

Plant good seeds so your foundation is strong and you are grounded and rooted in Me. Do not strive and drive to grow too fast. Your roots must be deep so your life with Me will be strong and long lasting. Many of My children run around doing this and doing that for Me without thinking of the consequences. They get weary and worn out in well doing. But remember this, My child: your roots will take time to grow, so be patient. Your fruit will reveal itself in due time.

Let your roots grow down into him and draw up nourishment from him. See that you go on growing in the LORD, and become strong and vigorous in the truth you were taught. Let your lives overflow with joy and thanksgiving for all he has done.

—Colossians 2:7 TLB

December 19

Everything you do affects others—either good or bad. All decisions you make will impact others. Do not think you have no responsibility in others' lives, whether they are your immediate family or generations to come.

Blessings and curses can affect you and your loved ones. Remember, your tongue is the rudder of the ship and can have a positive or negative effect on those in your life. My child, My precious one, choose blessing others and choose holiness over selfishness. It is the law of sowing and reaping. You will reap what you sow. Sow wisely.

> Sow for yourselves righteousness, reap the fruit of unfailing love, and break up your unplowed ground; for it is time to seek the LORD, until he comes and showers righteousness on you.
>
> —Hosea 10:12

December 20

You were created in My image. Remember, I took great care to knit you in your mother's womb. Every detail of who you are and who you will be was knitted together. Not one thing was left out. It took My utmost for your highest. Every stitch was delicately thought about, and it was all placed in your mother's womb for a purpose. I love to think of your uniqueness and your special creativity. Remember, your life is not to be wasted. It is My desire that you have a life that is radiant and passionate after Me. Bottom line: you were created for Me.

> For you created my inmost being; you knit me together in my mother's womb. I praise you because I am fearfully and wonderfully made; your works are wonderful, I know that full well.
>
> —Psalm 139:13–14

December 21

As this year begins to wind down, take time to reflect on the blessings. Many wonderful events have occurred over the year. My children are always blessed—they just forget sometimes to take an account of those blessings. Your life can get busy, but in the midst of all that busyness, you have spent much time with Me and I have revealed many jewels to you. Write them down and keep them in your heart. All you have learned and all you have received from Me will be used sometime in the future. Count on it. Nothing in My kingdom is wasted.

> As the rain and the snow come down from heaven, and do not return to it without watering the earth and making it bud and flourish, so that it yields seed for the sower and bread for the eater, so is my word that goes out from my mouth: It will not return to me empty, but will accomplish what I desire and achieve the purpose for which I sent it.
> —Isaiah 55:10–11

December 22

Stay healthy emotionally, physically, and spiritually. That is your mandate from Me. I need My bride to be ready and well prepared. Just as your body goes through physical changes the more you exercise and eat well, so are your emotional and spiritual lives affected in that same way. You are My temple, and My Spirit lives within you. Do not get lazy or lukewarm in any area of your life. The world needs what you have—to give away what I have given you, you must be in shape.

> Do you not know that your body is a temple of the Holy Spirit, who is in you, whom you have received from God? You are not your own; you were bought at a price. Therefore honor God with your body.
> —1 Corinthians 6:19–20

December 23

Take a deep breath and let Me fill you with My Spirit. Let Me fill those places that need a heavenly touch from your Father. Let Me embrace you with a Father's hug. Consider My ways and let Me guide you today. Make sure to listen to the quiet, still voice within you. Listen intently. Breathe in deeply My love for you and let it penetrate every cell of your body. It only takes a moment in time to connect with My heart and sense My presence.

> As the Father has loved me, so have I loved you. Now remain in my love. If you obey my commands, you will remain in my love, just as I have obeyed my Father's commands and remain in his love.
> —John 15:9–10

December 24

I came so that you may have life and live it to the fullest. I have poured out My Spirit upon you so you would live with all power and authority. My life was planned to bring you freedom in all areas of your life. There are mysteries I want to reveal to you that are in My Word and from My life here on earth. Connect your spirit with My Spirit so you can discern spiritual things. Do not let your flesh be your downfall. Rise up to a higher level.

> At that time Jesus said, "I praise you, Father, LORD of heaven and earth, because you have hidden these things from the wise and learned, and revealed them to little children. Yes, Father, for this was your good pleasure."
> —Matthew 11:25–26

December 25

Hope for the future and passion for life is yours today. This special day was planned from the beginning of time as a gift, a present, and a love offering to you and the world. Not everyone has received this gift of eternal life, but I came to destroy the enemy's works. Life with Me will be your biggest and greatest decision of all time. Begin afresh today and receive My love for you.

> For whoever finds me finds life and receives favor from the LORD.
> —Proverbs 8:35

December 26

I AM the light of the world. My face shines upon you and the Lord's glory has risen upon you. Let My light continually shine in your heart so the world will see and others will know My love. Light not only reveals the deep and hidden things but it illuminates the path and the journey to walk into peace and freedom. Many are looking for the way to happiness and joy. I AM the Way, the Truth, and the Life. Your life is evidence of My life in you. Remember, people will come to Me because of how you live and not based on what you say. So let your light shine brightly and do not hide it under a bushel.

> For God, who said, "Let light shine out of darkness," made his light shine in our hearts to give us the light of the knowledge of the glory of God in the face of Christ.
>
> —2 Corinthians 4:6

December 27

My child, My beloved one, walking alongside you has brought Me great joy. From the time I formed you in your mother's womb to where you are today brings Me great pleasure. You are flexible, pliable, and resilient and have persevered through it all. You have been strengthened in your weakness and you have continually kept praise in your heart. Oh, that all My children would know and understand the great depth of My love for them! When things got dark, you cried out for the light. When life was difficult, you looked for comfort and wisdom. You have done the best you know how to do. Rest, knowing I delight in you and will always be on your side.

> But the LORD stood at my side and gave me strength, so that through me the message might be fully proclaimed and all the Gentiles might hear it. And I was delivered from the lion's mouth.
>
> —2 Timothy 4:17

December 28

Expect great things today. Expect Me to move on your behalf. I AM working behind the scenes in ways you cannot see. Walk in that expectancy and open up your heart to receive. I love to bless you and shower My love upon you. The greatest is yet to come. Be assured of My plans and purposes in your life.

> May our LORD Jesus Christ himself and God our Father, who loved us and by his grace gave us eternal encouragement and good hope, encourage your hearts and strengthen you in every good deed and word.
>
> —2 Thessalonians 2:16–17

December 29

Stop and rest from this world's traditions. You are about to enter into a new season in life. A new year and a new adventure await you. I want you to search Me today for that next season. I have many things I want to say to you and show you about the days to come. No one goes into any battle unprepared without battle instructions and wisdom from on high. Whether you realize it or not, the enemy is crouching at the door and you must master it. You do this by submitting to Me and My plans. Know that it will be by My battle plan and not yours, so make sure to stop, rest, and listen for My voice.

> Prepare your shields, both large and small, and march out for battle! Harness the horses, mount the steeds! Take your positions with helmets on! Polish your spears, put on your armor!
>
> —Jeremiah 46:3–4

December 30

I AM doing a new thing in your life. Look and see what obstacles are robbing you of My blessings. Now is the time to remove any and all obstacles you face. You are called to rise above those circumstances like the bald eagle. The eagle doesn't go through a storm; it rises above it to the clear, calm skies. You can soar in the higher places and rest. There is always a better and more fruitful way to live, so do not let any obstacle stop you. Never give up, no matter what. Always rise above what you think tries to stop you.

But those who hope in the LORD will renew their strength. They will soar on wings like eagles; they will run and not grow weary, they will walk and not be faint.

—Isaiah 40:31

December 31

I have given you all authority and power. Never doubt your identity or inheritance. My heart breaks when My children don't walk in their God-given identity. You are not a victim but an overcomer! You are strong and mighty in Me, and nothing will ever block My love for you. Nothing can separate us. You have My incorruptible seed in you, and because of that, I AM part of you. There can be no corruption in those who live in Me. I want to manifest in and through you to a dying world so that they would know Me. I want to walk this journey with you because I have a plan, a purpose, and a hope for all who will call Me Lord. Let's keep walking!

In my vision at night I looked, and there before me was one like a son of man, coming with the clouds of heaven. He approached the Ancient of Days and was led into his presence. He was given authority, glory and sovereign power; all peoples, nations and men of every language worshiped him. His dominion is an everlasting dominion that will not pass away, and his kingdom is one that will never be destroyed.

—Daniel 7:13–14

KISS – Keep it simple stupid

LaVergne, TN USA
15 December 2010
208938LV00001B/2/P